Table of (

Inner Alchemy of Life:
Practical Magic for Bio-Hacking your Body with your
Neurotransmitters and Microbiota
Taylor Ellwood

Inner Alchemy of Life: Practical Magic for Bio-Hacking your Body with your Neurotransmitters and Microbiota
   by Taylor Ellwood
   © 2019 first edition

The right of Taylor Ellwood to be identified as the author of this work has been asserted by him in accordance with the Copyright, Designs and Patents Act, 1988.

Cover Art: Mark Reid
   Editor: Kat Bailey
   http://www.magicalexperiments.com

Other Non-Fiction Books by Taylor Ellwood

Pop Culture Magic 2.0
Pop Culture Magick
Pop Culture Magic Systems
Space/Time Magic Foundations
Inner Alchemy
Inner Alchemy of Life
Magical Identity
Manifesting Wealth
Magical Identity
The Book of Good Practices (With Bill Whitcomb)
Creating Magical Entities (With David Michael Cunningham & Amanda Wagener)
A Magical Life
Mystical Journeys
Magical Movements

Coming Soon

The Magic of Art
Inner Alchemy of Breath and Sound

Learn How Magic Works!

Free E-books available on my website Magicalexperiments.com

Whether you want a learn a simple 4 step process for creating a magical working, or discover how take your fandom and turn it into a spiritual practice, or learn simple breath meditations that enhance your life, or discover how to turn probabilities I have free e-books available for you that will teach you how magic works and how to get consistent results with it. Visit magicalexperiments.com/free-books[1] and download your free e-book today!

1.　http://www.magicalexperiments.com/free-books

Dedication

To R.J. Stewart and Anastacia Nutt with deepest respect for your work and the opportunities I've had to work with you. You are amazing people to know and work with and I am so grateful for your presence in my life!

Acknowledgements

I have had the great fortune to work with a number of people over the years on various magical experiments, including the work shared in this book. I want to thank Victoria Pike, Cate Anevski, Tony Marselle, Sara Sawyer, Colleen Chitty, Erik Roth, Annwyn Avalon, Amy Topham and many other people who have contributed to my magical work and practice with their insights and experiences. Special thanks to Cate Anevski for reading the initial manuscript and providing some suggestions for edits and clarification. When we can learn from each other, and keep open that's when we discover what magic can really be. And a special thank you to my dearest Kat whose love and support plays a significant role in the work I am able to do. Without her, I could not do it half so well.

Foreword

Inner Alchemy of Life is a continuation of the work I first described in *Inner Alchemy*, which I started developing when I was 20. At the age of 18 I was diagnosed with Bipolar 2 depression (manic depression). I had the option to take medicine, but I didn't want to because I didn't care for the side effects. I was certain I could discover a solution with magic. I was right.

When I was 20 I discovered two books that pointed me in the right direction: *Hands of Light* by Barbara Ann Brennan and *Programming the Human Biocomputer* by John Lilly. The first book was an energy work book that focused on healing. It is perhaps, even now, the best book on energy work I've found, and certainly the most comprehensive when it comes to applying energy work to healing the body.

The author of *Hands of Light* referenced *Programming the Human Biocomputer*, which sparked my interest to read it. She also provided a meditation technique based off her work with the book. I read *Programming the Human Biocomputer* and immediately saw why the other author had referenced and used it, because in that book John Lilly explores the possibilities of working with your body, specifically your neurochemical states of being.

I took what I learned in both books and tried the meditation technique with the goal being that I would alter my neurochemistry and change the predisposition to depression. I went in, via meditation, to my brain and reprogrammed it so my Serotonin would stay longer in my brain. That was all it took to change my brain chemistry and my life. I no longer got depressed because of the neurochemistry of my brain. Note: I still get depressed on occasion, but it doesn't last long and it's an appropriate response to environmental stresses such as a really bad day or something along those lines, whereas before my change it was literally a state of being that would last weeks, months, you get the idea.

At the time I was satisfied with the result and the working, but I eventually began to wonder if it was possible to do more with the body than what had been described in those books. While both of the aforementioned books were helpful, what I realized is that they were just a starting point. However there wasn't any other work out there, magically, that dealt with working with the body in a comprehensive way that allowed someone to change their neurochemistry. Even to this day there are very few books that approach working with the body magically, and usually those books are focused on working with the fluids of the body, such as blood or cum.

A few years after I'd changed my neurochemistry, I decided to start experimenting more with my body. I felt there was more to discover and that magically people were missing out. My experiments with the body ranged from working with the fluids of the body to working with the cells, neurotransmitters, bacteria, and even DNA of the body. The body is a universe in its own right, and that's what my initial work revealed to me. To read about that work, I invite you to pick up my book *Inner Alchemy*, where I discuss it in depth.

Since writing *Inner Alchemy* I've continued my experiments with the body. I shared some of the evolutions of that work in *Magical Identity*, but after writing that book I realized that I needed to put together an entire book that just focused on this subject in order to give it the full attention it deserves.

The Inner Alchemy of Life is that book. I've written it to share my ongoing work with the body, specifically the microbiota and neurochemistry of the body, so that you can hopefully explore this work as well. This book is partially a grimoire and partially a practical manual that describes magical work you can do with the universe that is your body. The grimoire aspect focuses on describing the neurotransmitters, bacteria, and other forms of life that exist in the human body and are essential if the body is to actually have life. The practical aspect focuses on describing the methods and techniques I've developed to work with spirits of the body, so that you can replicate and, more importantly, experiment with the techniques. It is focused on working with the spirits of the body but there is much more to explore about the body, which I will share in a future book.

I am one of the very few people I know who has worked with the body in the way I describe in this book. Everyone else I know doing this work has learned it from me.

It's my fervent hope and desire that more people will take up this work. I've always been ahead of the times I live in, in terms of my writing. I wrote *Pop Culture Magick* over a decade ago and it's only in the last couple of years (at the time of this writing) that people have finally caught up and started exploring it and working with it. I am curious to see if the same will apply to my work in space/time magic and with the inner alchemical work I'm presenting here.

Regardless of whether that happens or not, this work is being written and shared because we need to change the relationships we have with our bodies and the life within our bodies. I feel this inner alchemical work is a potential key to the continued evolution of humans, and just as importantly a way to enter into a better relationship with life around us. In doing this work what you discover is a different relationship not just with your body, but with life in general.

Taylor Ellwood
Portland, Oregon
November, 2018

Chapter 1: A Brief Introduction to Your Body

We, you and me, take our bodies granted for every day. I know that's a bold statement to start a book with, yet I'm making it for a specific reason. The human body is taken for granted precisely because we live with it every day and because our sense of self encompasses our experience of the body to the point that we ignore the actual reality of the body.

The actual reality of the body isn't the singular identity we typically operate under, but something much different. Your body is comprised of millions upon millions of life forms that are essential for keeping your body alive. When you look in the mirror, you can't see those life forms. All you see is your face and your body. What you project on body is your identity, and that serves a useful purpose in terms of helping you navigate everyday life, but it also, in a way, divorces you from the reality of your body.

On occasion you'll be forcefully reminded of the reality of your body, usually when you're sick or in some other situation where your body fundamentally needs to do something more than just help you maintain the illusion of a singular self. When you are sick, you intimately experience your body fighting bacteria or viruses that are not part of the body. The temperature of your body rises in order to make the body less hospitable to the invaders, and you may end up vomiting and hacking and otherwise expelling the invader. Still, that experience only gives you a taste of the reality of your body and you usually aren't able to fully appreciate it at the time.

When you exercise or have sex you might also experience the body differently as the neurotransmitters respond to whatever you're doing and flood your body and brain with the appropriate neurochemicals, but again the experience you have will be filtered through your identity and you likely won't fully recognize what's going on. You'll hopefully enjoy the experience, though.

Why is it important to understand the body?

Now it can be argued that it's not really important that you know what's going on behind the scenes with your body. After all, if it ain't broke, why fix it? However, I think we do ourselves and the life within our bodies a disservice when we don't really know what's going on and show no inquisitiveness to discover what's going on. It is also much harder to heal your body when you don't actually understand what is happening on the cellular level.

In general, I've noticed that people take the approach of ignoring the body, treating it as an unwanted encumbrance, or filtering it through the perceptions of the sense of self. One of the reasons this occurs is because of the cultural and religious baggage that so many of us carry. We've been taught that the body is sinful and dirty and that it causes us to feel urges we shouldn't give into. The counter response to that meme has been a hedonic plunge into the pleasures of the body via sex, BDSM, and entheogens, but that approach is also problematic because it doesn't truly embrace the body, so much as it tries to saturate our identity with pleasure. Now there's nothing wrong with experiencing pleasure per se, but when no sense of moderation is applied it can lead to some unpleasant consequences.

When you look at how people approach the health of the body you see attempts to medicate it through drugs (often with disastrous side effects), through invasive surgeries, or to heal it through working with the energy of the body. All of these approaches can be effective to a certain degree, but what is lacking is a comprehensive way of communicating with the life within your body in order to enlist its aid and also to discover what you can be doing to help its efforts.

As an example, when people discuss doing energy work to heal someone, the approach that is taken is very generalized. The reason for that is because the healer is focused on the identity of the person as opposed to healing the actual issue. So if a person has a broken leg they'll send energy to help heal the leg, but they won't necessarily focus on the specifics that might be involved in such a situation. They won't consider working with the bone marrow or bone, the blood cells or the muscles. Instead energy is thrown at it, much like you might throw spaghetti at a wall in the hopes that it sticks. Such an approach to healing is ultimately clumsy because you aren't working with the specific areas of the body that need help nor are you enlisting the aid of the life within the body that can help with more focused healing work.

What stops practitioners from getting more detailed is the thought that they might have to learn anatomy, biology, or neuroscience in order to even begin working on that level with the body. However, while I think it is useful to learn some anatomy, biology and neuroscience, I don't think you absolutely need to have an in-depth knowledge of those subjects in order to work with your body or the life within it. In fact, I have learned some knowledge of anatomy or biology or neuroscience, but not enough that it would make me a biologist or neuro-scientist. My point being that some knowledge is useful, but don't let what you don't know stop you from discovering or experiencing the miracles of the body. What you need is a willingness to get to know your body and the life within it better. And while some book knowledge can help with that, ultimately the way you get to know your body better is to actually work with it and the life within it.

With that in mind, I want to share with you some perspectives about the body that can be helpful in showing you how to get to know your body without necessarily learning a ton about anatomy or biology. In the foreword, I shared my story of how I modified my neurochemistry because of reading Brennan and Lilly's works and trying out the concepts, but my interest in working with my body magically continued to expand as a result of reading the Dune series. I was fascinated by how the Bene Gesserit could control their body chemistry and I wondered if it was actually possible. The work I did using Brennan's meditation technique and Lilly's concepts of programming the brain told me it was possible, but I was certain that a person could go much deeper. That, however, would require a different kind of conscious connection with the body and even with how we relate to the body. In order to develop that consciousness connection I needed to explore a variety of perspectives and techniques, all of which contributed to the development of my own work with the body and the life within it. With that in mind I want to share those perspectives with you so you can do your own research. Please keep in mind that while I have provided you everything you need in this book to do the work, learning about and exploring what I share below can certainly help you as well.

Taoist breathing meditation techniques have played a significant role in helping me to connect with my body. The techniques I've found most useful for this work I discovered by reading and working through B. K. Frantzis's books, which focus on teaching you how to dissolve internal blockages and connect with your chi. Note: You don't need to use Taoist meditation to do this, but you do need some type of body centric meditation practice. I find that these practices also teach you how to connect more intimately with your body. As you dissolve the tensions and stress that your body carries, you free up emotional blockages and simultaneously begin to discover how you've repressed your body's attempt to communicate with you through the very symptoms of pain and stress we carry with us every day.

Additionally, I find cultivating a sensual conscious awareness of the body can also be useful for working with the neurotransmitters and microbial life, because what you must learn is how to pay attention to how your body is communicating with you on multiple levels. A sensual awareness begins to teach you how to listen to your body. Not surprisingly, though it is hard for people to cultivate such awareness due to how we've been taught to relate to the body and, for that matter, to the world around us. We've been taught to suppress and ignore the more subtle forms of communication in favor of humancentric communication. In order to work with your body, however, you must embrace the sensual awareness and use it as a gateway that leads you deeper into the universe that is your body.

So how do you do this? By cultivating your senses of perception and applying them both to the world around you and within you. Perception is treated as passive activity, but it is actually participatory, calling on a person to engage in the world, "By asserting that perception is inherently participatory, we mean that perception always involves, at its most intimate level, the experience of an active interplay, or coupling, between the perceiving body and that which it perceives. Prior to all verbal reflections, at the level of our spontaneous, sensorial engagement with the world around us, we are all animists" (Abram 1997, p. 57). We can use sensual awareness to help us shift out of ordinary consciousness we normally inhabit, which is primarily concept driven. When we do this it allows us to engage life on its level of consciousness. Whether that's connecting with a plant, animal, or blood cell, what is required is that we shift toward an experiential perception that opens us to being curious and receptive instead of conceptually categorizing everything (Shusterman 2012). The way we do this is by stepping outside of our own language and instead using our senses to help us connect and communicate experientially. We pay attention to our senses and let them speak to us, unfiltered by language. Meditation can be helpful for this kind of activity, but so can simply paying attention to the sensations you experience and being present with them, without having to filter them through language.

Cultivating the perception of your body also opens you to discovering the rhythms of the body and the way those rhythms set up the experience you have with your body (Schusterman 2012). Our experience of the body is, in a sense, static. We don't always realize that throughout the day the temperature of the human body changes, that our sense of wakefulness and sleepiness is driven by circadian rhythms and that the various microbes, hormones, neurotransmitters, etc. in our bodies perform a variety of roles that creates the experiences we have each day and take for granted (Ackerman 2007). We, at best, have a crude awareness of this rhythm driven by the needs to eat or go to bathroom or sleep, but we can refine that awareness by paying closer attention to the subtle signals our bodies send us throughout the day. Such subtle signals can be found in the shift of your temperature or the feeling of your stomach knotting as it responds to your emotions. It can the feeling of your heart racing or the subtle motions of your digestive track working to move food through it. It can also be the choice to be present with feelings of pain, without necessarily trying to get rid of them. For example, the physical pain you feel can sometimes connect with a deeper narrative rooted in your emotions such as anxiety, anger and depression, or through feelings of stress. When we suppress that physical pain we are essentially blocking out something that the body is trying to communicate to us. But if we do the opposite and open ourselves up to what we feel physically, it can provide us valuable insights to what we are working through emotionally and mentally as well (Mindell 2002, Mindell 2002, Schusterman 2012). Doing this won't automatically heal the pain or cure the issue, but it may provide you valuable insights and even closure because you've chosen to listen to your body and be receptive to the messages it provides you: "I still amplify their pain and people feel better, living their diseases because then their disease becomes a meaningful experience that is constantly pressing them toward consciousness. It wakes them up" (Mindell 2002 P. 5). The choice to wake up, to be present with your body in health and in illness is a choice that allows you not only to connect more meaningfully with your body, but also communicate with it using conscious intent.

Learning to connect with my body through the pain it shares with me has helped me make dietary and exercise changes that couldn't have happened if I simply repressed my symptoms. Granted, the choice to connect with your body won't heal all your pain. But it may make it easier to connect and work through a disease or chronic issue you have. In addition, doing this kind of practice where you open your awareness to your body and let it instruct you can help you open yourself to other experiences:

> Body language is like dream language. It gives you indications that the conscious mind is not yet able to give. Once the mind is able to function in harmony with the body signals, the body automatically relaxes. If the body is tense, there is reason. The tension is needed, and shouldn't be arbitrarily relaxed. If you can find and integrate the processes in apparently lethal symptoms, powerful dreams, and strange acts of fate, you normally feel better and you have more energy. Yet you will also find that the new behavior not only widens your personality but often brings you to the limits of what you can do. (Mindell 2002 P. 21).

When we pair this awareness of tension with meditation we can unlock the language of the body, especially in regards to what it is trying to tell us. At the same time, we need to be open to how the body may switch its communication with us. A person's initial experience may be a feeling of tension that then becomes a vibration of sound or a visualization, or even a smell or taste that provides some further insights, if we are open to those insights (Frantzis 2001, Mindell 2002). Additionally, part of cultivating your consciousness awareness of your body involves paying attention to region-centric experiences of the body. A feeling of neck pain can speak as much to issues of over conceptualization and an inability to connect with body as to just being an actual pain in the neck. Likewise a pain in your heart region can help you work through an inability to feel emotions as well as be an actual pain that needs to be looked into (Mindell 2002). The point here is that what you experience in your body should be carefully felt and acknowledged both in terms of the physical implications of what you feel, and the possible emotional and mental narratives that can be explored. Don't assume that because you feel pain in your heart it's only related to emotional issues. Get it checked out, but be open to the idea that the physical pain can be a doorway to experiencing a deeper message that your body wants you to pay attention to. I will be exploring these concepts in deeper depth in my forthcoming book The Inner Alchemy of Breath and Sound.

Exercise

What can you do to open yourself to experiencing your body with a different level of perspective? First, I would suggest doing some meditation breathing, but pay attention in particular to the sensations of your body. Secondly, the next time you feel a physical sensation of pain or uneasiness or anything else, open your mind to fully experiencing it and be open to whatever information or experiences you get. Do this on a regular basis and you'll notice a real difference in not only how you relate to your body, but also the world around you. You may even find you change habits and behaviors as a result.

The Neuro-Biology of Body Consciousness

There is also of course the additional layer of body consciousness to explore, the one which this book explores in depth: The connection with the microbial life, the neurotransmitters, hormones, and other aspects of the biological and neural chemistry that make us what we are. I mentioned earlier that you don't have to have an in-depth knowledge of anatomy or biology or neuroscience, but it doesn't hurt to acquire some knowledge that can help us in our efforts to connect with our bodies, and the life within them, more consciously.

The first thing we need to understand is that there's a difference between microbial life and neurotransmitters, hormones, and amino acids. The latter grouping is responsible for the nutrients in our bodies and play a role in our everyday experience of life. For example, neurotransmitters play a role in the emotions you feel, how awake or sleepy you are, etc. Microbial life, on the other hand, are bacteria, Archaea, Protozoa, etc. who live in our bodies. They live in a symbiotic relationship with us that provides benefits to us and to them. Not all microbial life is friendly to us, which is why we sometimes get bacterial infections and fevers, and can even die, but the fact is we also host microbial life that plays an essential role in keeping us alive. If we didn't have microbial life in us we couldn't digest food very easily, process waste, or have a number of other functions fulfilled that are provided for us by the life that lives within us (Ackerman 2007, Maczulak 2011, Blaser 2014).

In this book we'll be working with both the microbial life, the cells of the body, the neurochemicals and hormones. It's important to make the distinction I've made above because they aren't all one and the same, and as a result you may discover that how you work with one type of body entity may differ from how you work with another. Nonetheless, what we'll also discover is how the cells of our bodies communicate and how everything works together. We'll even see that there's a strong possibility that a person's chi is actually the life energy and information that is passed through the cells and microbial life: "Biologists have concluded that the molecules of living organism have the capacity to store and transmit information by means of their reactions. This constant communication between biological molecules allows the correct functioning of the cells" (Tibika 2013, p. 66). If we consider that the correct functioning of cells is caused by regular communication between the cells, we also need to consider what that communication looks like. Tibika notes that biologists think that this communication happens by how cells react to each other:

> These interactions can be conceived as the meeting of two molecules with complex structures: one that has the shape of a 'lock' and the other the shape of a 'key'. Only when the key comes into contact with the right lock does a reaction

take place and information is transmitted. In other words, the information carried by one molecule is transmitted to another only when this molecule has been 'identified' by its structure. This arrangement ensures the selectivity necessary to maintain order between constantly reacting molecules. (Tibika 2013, P. 67).

Our own work, as a result, has to factor in this communication, which is one of the reasons anthropomorphic approaches to working with your body are ultimately very limited. We have to find a way to experientially communicate with the cells, microbiota, and neurotransmitters using their communication. Breath work, where we cultivate chi or energy, can be part of that process, the gateway to accessing that experiential level of communication.

What we need to also understand is that this process of communication works across all levels of the body. The neurotransmitters in the brain respond in a similar way to the receptors in the brain as the cells in the rest of the body respond to each other. So what we have is a communication network in our own body that responds and signals and generates the experiences we have at the level of our consciousness, all without that consciousness really needing to do anything (Ratey 2001, LeDoux 2002, Lipton 2005).

Naturally a question that might be asked is, "Taylor, if the body takes care of itself, why even do all this work?" And the answer is that while the body can and does take care of itself, sometimes it doesn't and there is faulty wiring. In my case there was faulty wiring, which resulted in having manic-depressive episodes. That changed when I adjusted my neurochemistry and it made me realize that if I could do something like that, I could likely do a lot more. I'm never one to settle for less, and if you're reading this book I'm presuming you aren't willing to settle for less either, so it makes sense that while the body can do a lot, we must do our part to take better care of ourselves and to recognize that we have an obligation to the life that supports us; that we support it in turn.

Over the years, my work with my body has caused me to pay much closer attention to the signals it sends and has resulted in me making changes to my diet, exercise, and overall lifestyle. So many people are out of touch with their bodies so they don't learn how to listen or communicate with the body, but once you start doing that it changes your relationship with yourself. It's my hope that this book will help you do that.

In the back of this book you'll find the bibliography, which can help you if you want to discover what other people have written on these topics, but what I hope you will do is continue reading this book and doing the exercises in it. That will help you begin to discover and work with the universe of your body in context to healing work you might wish to do, but also in discovering what your body really can be, if you work with it on a conscious level. The work you do here can apply to working with other people as well, but I suggest focusing first on yourself.

Where do we begin?

I want you to take a moment and go look at yourself in the mirror. In the mirror what you see is how people typically think of their body. You see your face, hair, skin, arms, legs, hands, feet, and torso. However what you're seeing is only the outward appearance of your body.

Now take a moment and put your fingers on your neck or wrist until you feel a pulse. That pulse is your heart beating. You can't see your heart, but you can feel it working away to keep you alive. Most of the time we don't think about our heart because we don't pay attention to the heart beat. We might notice it if we've exercised or if we visit the doctor, but otherwise we don't pay attention to the heart beat.

Take a deep breath. Pay attention to how your lungs and diaphragm expand and contract. Take another breath and pay attention again. Usually you don't think about how you breathe unless you're meditating, someone calls attention to it, or you're sick (because congestion can change how you breathe).

Put your hand on your stomach. Do you feel or hear a rumble? If you've just eaten your food is being digested and if you haven't eaten for a while you might be feeling hungry. Take a moment and really allow yourself to feel that digestion or hunger. Again this a sensation you probably don't think much about, beyond recognizing you feel hungry or full.

The next time you need to use the bathroom, pay attention to the sensations you feel at that time. The need to pee or poop is a signal that helps you get rid of waste your body has processed. You likely don't think of it much when it happens, but that feeling of needing to pee or poop is your body's way of signaling you to make sure it happens.

Every day you experience these sensations and others and you probably don't spare much time to think about them. The body is running itself so you can do what you do. However if you pay attention to these sensations you can learn a lot about your body and how your body takes care of itself. Perhaps the most important lesson you can learn is that your body is much more than just what you see in the mirror. Yet even those sensations I've had you pay attention to are just the tip of the iceberg.

Inside your body there is activity occurring that you aren't even aware of. Your cells are communicating with each other, bacteria is helping your body digest and process waste and neurotransmitters and hormones are responding to what you and your body are experiencing. Some of the sensations I've described above are the results of the activity, but in some cases you might not even feel something, yet nonetheless something is happening.

The question then is how do we connect to that activity and to what is performing that activity if we aren't even aware of it. The answer is magic. Magic is what allows us to find a way to connect with the activity and the life responsible for that activity. With magic we can form a different relationship with the microbial life inside of us, a conscious relationship where we work together. With magic, we can connect with our neurotransmitters and amino acids and work with them to enhance our quality of life. The reason we may wish to do that is because it enables us to be proactive in regards to the health of the body, and also opens us to experience not only our body, but the world around us from different perspectives. Those perspectives are needed, because they may just help us change how we live in the world and how we treat it.

The Magic involved in working with the body

In chapter 2, we're going to explore the theory behind the magical work you'll do in this book, and in chapter 3 I'll share the actual exercises you'll be doing. However, a brief overview is useful because it allows us to appreciate all the moving parts involved in doing this work. We will be using a few different techniques in this book.

The first technique is meditation. We'll use breathing meditation as the gateway into the body. Your breath really is the door to creation for your body. You breathe in and out every day countless times and your breath creates a rhythm you can use to connect to the internal rhythms of your body.

The second technique we'll be using is pathworking. Pathworking will allow us to connect to the consciousness of the various lifeforms in our body and create a means for us to communicate with them. That communication is essential if we are to have a conscious relationship with our bodies and if we're to do health magic.

The third technique we'll be using is the Alphabet of Desire. Austin Osman Spare developed this technique as a way to create a personalized system of correspondence for whatever magical work you are doing. Later in this book I'll share my alphabet of desire for the work I've done to connect with the body, but I would also urge you to create your own alphabet of desire. Doing that will help you establish a meaningful and deep connection with your body and the life within it.

All of these techniques combined will help you develop your system of magic around working with the life in your body. What will help you get the most out of this book is doing the work and recording what happens so that you can modify and tweak what you're learning here to make it fit your needs and magical work.

Conclusion

You've now got an overview of what this book is about and what we'll be working on in it. I invite you to keep an open mind, but also to test everything I share here. As with my other works, what I ultimately hope for is that you'll make what you learn here your own. If you can develop a personalized system of magic that helps you connect with your body and helps you to work with it magically then this book will have served its purpose. So let's get started on fleshing out the theory of what's involved in this process.

Chapter 2: The Theory behind the Inner Alchemy of Life

Working with the body isn't just a matter of deciding you'll connect with the microbial life or neurotransmitters, but is also about developing a relationship of respect and understanding of what you are working with, especially since what you work with lives within you and is responsible for keeping you alive and healthy. You want to make the effort to do some research about what you're connecting with. I've always found Wikipedia to be a useful resource for looking up information about bacteria and neurotransmitters, but I also recommend reading some books on the topic.

But research alone isn't enough. Ultimately you'll create the relationships with the neurotransmitters and bacteria by actually having direct experiences with them. You will let them instruct you in what they are and what they do, as well as how you can best work with them. To get that started we need to learn how to direct our conscious awareness inward, to the body.

The majority of people aren't used to directing their conscious awareness inward. Even in meditation the focus on the body is more of a byproduct of the meditation, because you're using your body to identify places where you feel physical and emotional tension and stress. What we want to do is intentionally direct our awareness into the body, in order to know the body.

In this case knowing the body involves allowing your consciousness to become part of the bodily processes that you can't see or even feel. For example, one of the very first workings you'll be doing is learning how to become a blood cell. It isn't something we normally think about, but your blood is basically the highway of your body, so it makes sense to become a blood cell in order to travel to different parts of your body.

The breathing meditation we use is simple and designed to help you go into your body and immerse your consciousness in your body so that you can connect with the desired neurotransmitters and bacteria. Alternately, you can also use this meditation to become an organ in your body, which also can be useful for this work. Once you are comfortable with the meditation we incorporate pathworking. There are two types of pathworking we'll be using: anthropomorphic and non-anthropomorphic pathworking.

Anthropomorphic Pathworking

The anthropomorphic pathworking is primarily used as a way to help ease you into connecting with neurotransmitters, bacteria and everything else we'll be working with. I developed it when I first began to explore what it might be like to work with neurotransmitters. The way it works is that you basically ask the neurotransmitter or bacteria to appear before you in a form you can recognize and tell you what its function is, as well as how you can work with it. You also ask it for a symbol that you can use to connect with it in the future.

The neurotransmitter or bacteria will show up in a form that is familiar to you. For example, when I first worked with Serotonin, it showed up as a 6 eyed red snake. For other people, Serotonin showed up as a duck or a woman. My point in sharing that with you is that the neurotransmitter/bacteria will show up in whatever form is familiar for you.

When the neurotransmitter/bacteria speaks to you, it will use your language to communicate with you and tell you about what it does and how it can work with you. This is primarily being done as a way to help you understand how to work with the neurotransmitter.

You use this working to get the neurotransmitter or bacteria to share a sensation with you. That sensation will be used in the non-anthropomorphic working to help you develop an experiential working relationship.

The anthropomorphic pathworking is useful when you're first starting to work with neurotransmitters and bacteria or the body in general, but it's my hope that you'll eventually no longer need to use it. The one problem with this technique is that it is anthropomorphic, which means that it frames the experience in a humancentric context. This is why the neurotransmitter/bacteria appears before you in a form you are comfortable with and speaks in your language. It's useful in the short term, but a crutch, in the long term.

Non-Anthropomorphic Pathworking

The non-anthropomorphic pathworking is experiential. The focus is on using the direct sensations you feel and experience as a way to connect with the neurotransmitter or bacteria. This is the technique we want to graduate to, because it allows us to develop a much deeper connection with the bacteria and neurotransmitters. It's also how we figure out if something is off with the body because we also develop a deeper relationship with the body in general.

Your body communicates with you every day, but usually people learn to ignore or suppress the communication, or only pay attention when they are to a point where they don't feel good. I want to help you change your relationship with your body so that you are mindfully communicating with it and the life within you, and as a result taking actions that keep you healthy.

With the non-anthropomorphic pathworking we travel into our bodies and use the sensation we associate with a given neurotransmitter or microbiota to connect with it. We've gotten that sensation from our initial working, and we're using it as an introduction to the experiential communication that needs to happen. When you use the sensation, you want to allow it to take over your experience of the meditation so the neurotransmitter or bacteria can communicate with you through the sensations.

After you finish with the meditation, you want to take your memory of the sensation and translate it into a visual symbol. The visual symbol is part of your alphabet of desire, and it allows you to connect to the sensation and neurotransmitter/bacteria, which can be helpful when you're doing work to either deepen your relationship with the body spirits or if you're doing specific work around your health and want to bring the body spirits into that work.

The Alphabet of Desire

The alphabet of desire is a technique that Austin Osman Spare developed to create a series of visual symbols that are connected to spirits and to each other:

> Each 'letter' represents a power...an unconscious structure or a variety of energy that the sorcerer recognizes or wishes to recognize within his deep psyche. The letter acts as a way of designating the nature of this force, even while one's rational mind is left in the dark. By encouraging his deep psyche to design this alphabet, the wizard creates his own personal system of symbols, compact images he can use to call up the power to change his consciousness or charge his sigils. (Mace 1984, P. 34).

The benefit of the alphabet is that it allows you to create personalized symbols/sigils that connect to the spirits you're working with. It also enables you to call up that connection through the symbol, instead of having to do a convoluted magical working.

In context to this work, the alphabet of desire you are developing embodies the experiential relationships you have with the spirits of the body. Each sigil represents a specific relationship and you can use the sigil to call up that relationship. You can also use multiple sigils to call multiple spirits up and then work with them collaboratively. We use this technique also as a way to provide a visual medium that we can use to lead us back into the direct experience of the sensations.

Conclusion

In the next chapter I'll walk you through the actual practices you'll be using to do this work. These techniques have been tested by myself and other people over the lifetime of my work with neurotransmitters and microbiota and they are quite useful for helping develop a relationship with the spirits of your body.

The reason I've opted to present the theory and practice separately is that I find a scaffolded approach to be most effective when learning magic. The theory provides you the concepts and allows you to get comfortable with the work. Now we step into actually doing the work and as you'll discover it's when you do the work that you actually come to know it...because experience is the best teacher.

Chapter 3: The Practical Techniques of the Inner Alchemy of Life

We've covered the theory. Now it's time to get practical, so from here on out, what will make this book most effective is if you actually do the work. Each technique presented here builds on the previous technique. I recommend working with each one until you don't have to think about it, but can simply do it. We'll start with the breathing meditation, which you'll be using for the purpose of directing your conscious awareness to connect with your body.

Touch the tip of your tongue to the roof of your mouth. You'll do this to stop yourself from breathing in and out through your mouth and also because when you touch your tongue to the roof of your mouth it connects the front and back chi channels of the body together which unlocks your consciousness.

Take a deep breath, inhaling through your nose. When you exhale, also breathe out through your nose. For the first few breaths, simply focusing on being aware of your breathing. As you relax into the breathing, let your consciousness flow into your body, becoming more and more focused on the body.

Continue breathing and let your consciousness become smaller and smaller, until you become part of your bloodstream. When you merge your consciousness with the bloodstream, for all intents and purposes you are using your blood to connect with any other part of your body and then transmitting your consciousness to that part of your body. You can think of your blood as the information super highway of the body.

When you visit an organ of your body you can expand your consciousness to merge with the organ and then ask the organ to share information with you. For example, if you were to connect with your kidneys or liver then you could discover what that organ might want to communicate with you.

You can also use this body traveling technique to take you to parts of your body such as the brain or hormone glands which produce neurotransmitters and hormones or to the stomach, skin, and other places of the body where bacteria resides. In either case, you then perform a pathworking, so let's explore both pathworkings.

Organ Pathworking

If you choose to connect with an organ you would use your blood to carry your consciousness to the organ of choice, and then merge your consciousness with your organ. The merging of your consciousness involves taking on and becoming the organ, making it your identity. The benefit of doing this practice is that it not only helps you learn more about the organ, but it can possibly help you identify potential issues with it. It might surprise you, but we can actually feel our internal organs. We've just learned to tune that feeling out and make it into a part of our general body sensation. But when you connect with an organ you can single out that organ and how it feels and that can help you communicate with the organ.

You can take two approaches to connecting with the organ. The first (anthropomorphic) approach is to ask the organ to appear before you in a form that is familiar to you and ask it to communicate with you in your spoken language. This can be useful as an initial means of connection but shouldn't be relied upon for long term communication with an organ of your body.

The second (non-anthropomorphic) approach involves settling into the feeling of the organ and allowing that feeling to communicate with you. When you take this approach, you simply want to feel the organ without trying to interpret the feeling. Let the feeling wash over you and share with your consciousness what the organs needs you to know. You'll find out a lot of information through the feeling.

For example, when I did this organ working with my kidneys, the feeling I got from my kidneys made it clear that I needed to change my diet. Subsequent changes created improvements for me when using the bathroom. When we connect with our organs intentionally we can learn a lot about our body and what we can do to take better care of it.

Our organs can also help on an emotional level. When I did the pathworking with my liver, the liver helped me recognize my relationship with anger needed to change if I didn't want that relationship to have an adverse effect on my liver. I did some work with my anger and noticed that my liver afterwards felt different.

While the main focus of this book is to work with the neurotransmitters and bacteria of the body, I can't state enough how important it is to also connect with the organs in your body and discover what they have to share with you. I've been able to make some substantial changes to how I manage my health because of how I've connected to the organs of my body, specifically through melding my consciousness with them and letting them communicate with me through the feelings that result.

Neurotransmitter/Bacteria Pathworking (Anthropomorphic)

The anthropomorphic version of the neurotransmitter/microbiota work is primarily used as an introduction to whatever you're working with. Using the meditation where you merge with the blood cell you use the blood to take you where the neurotransmitter or bacteria would be located in the body. For instance, if you're working with Tyrosine, a neurotransmitter, you'll travel to the brain. If you're working with Stomach Bacteria, you'll travel to your intestines. The research you do on a given neurotransmitter or bacteria will help you figure out where you need to direct your consciousness. Keep in mind that some neurotransmitters also show up in your body, so you won't always work with them in your brain.

When you travel to the specific part of your body where you'll meet the spirit, mentally call out to it and ask it to appear before you in a form you can interact with. You may need to call out several times and you can do this vocally as well if it helps you in connecting with the spirit. The neurotransmitter or bacteria will then appear in a form you can connect with. For instance, when I did this working with Serotonin, it appeared as a six eyed red snake. My gut bacteria appeared as a girl with yellow moving hair. Your version will likely look different, being what's relevant to you.

After the neurotransmitter or bacteria spirit appears, ask it to tell you about what it does for the body. Pay close attention to the information shared, because you'll use that information to verify that you've connected with the spirit. What I and other people have noticed is that typically the spirit will use your first language to communicate.

After the spirit has shared its information with you ask it for a symbol. The neurotransmitter or bacteria will usually give you a visual symbol but may use tactile sensations, so pay close attention to what you visualize or feel. Once you have the symbol thank it and end your meditation.

Afterwards you'll want to verify the information you've been given, so my suggestion is to do some online research via Wikipedia, which actually has accurate information about what a given neurotransmitter or microbiota does. In the bibliography, I include some useful books to draw on, but Wikipedia and nimh.nih.gov are useful resources that provide an overview. I do recommend being thorough and doing your research. Once you've verified the information, you can then do the next part of this meditation.

The second part of this meditation involves using the symbol the neurotransmitter/bacteria gave you to connect with it more directly. The benefit of doing this is that you get a sense of how the neurotransmitter/bacteria actually feels. Do the breathing meditation until you connect your consciousness with your body. Then visualize the symbol, call to the neurotransmitter or bacteria, and allow your consciousness to merge with it. Open yourself to whatever sensations come up. These sensations are the physical experience of the neurotransmitter or microbiota working in your body. This is also your introduction to the non-anthropomorphic experience, because you're not trying to communicate with the spirit using your language or the form it appeared in, but instead you're opening yourself to experiencing the sensation of the neurotransmitter or bacteria. Allow yourself to be present with that sensation for as long as is comfortable and then end the meditation and record your results.

Now you might wonder at this point why you even need to do the non-anthropomorphic working, if what I've shared above allows you to connect with the neurotransmitter or microbiota. And that's a fair question to ask. The reason we want to do non-anthropomorphic workings with the neurotransmitters and microbiota is that it will allow us to deepen the connection even further and get used to communicating with the neurotransmitter and microbiota experientially. It will also help us do more advanced work with these spirits, which is important if you want to work with them on your body.

Neurotransmitter/Bacteria Non-Anthropomorphic Pathworking

For this meditation you are using the previous experience you had with the neurotransmitter or bacteria as a springboard to connect even more deeply with the spirit on an experiential level. For this working you do NOT want to use the symbol you were given. Instead you're going to rely on the actual sensory experience you had to be your guide. You also won't be vocally calling out to the neurotransmitter or bacteria. You're just using the physical sensation to connect with it.

By now you've already had a sensory experience. When you go into your meditation what you want to do is draw on the memory of the experience and use it to invoke the spirit you'll work with. Alternately you can also focus your awareness on your body, particularly where the neurotransmitter or bacteria is located and use the physical feelings you sense to help you connect with the neurotransmitter/bacteria. For example, if I want to work with Stomach Bacteria, I might either try to connect with them when I'm feeling hungry or right after I've eaten a meal. By using the physical sensations I'm feeling in my stomach as a guide, I can connect with the bacteria experientially.

When you connect with the spirit on an experiential level you're not asking it to appear before you in a form you are familiar with, or communicate with you using your language. Instead you are allowing the experience itself to be the communication. Open yourself up to the feelings and sensations you experience and allow it to carry you deeper into the connection you have with the neurotransmitter or bacteria. The sensations will help you identify and recognize the way the neurotransmitter or bacteria communicates with your body, which can be useful for purposely activating them or deactivating them as needed.

Something to keep in mind is that when you do this type of experiential meditation you're not necessarily trying to say something back. What you're doing is soaking in the experience and using it as a guide to help you call up the experience when you need it. For example, the experience of Epinephrine can be used to help dull pain, which is good for a situation where you've been injured.

Creating your Alphabet of Desire

When you come out of the meditation, you may wish to draw the sensations you've felt. The drawing will become the symbol in your alphabet of desire that allows you to call up that experience as needed, whenever you want to directly work with the neurotransmitter or bacteria. The symbol will also be useful if you want to work with multiple neurotransmitters and bacteria at the same time.

When I did these meditations I would do the drawing and then later use it to experience the sensation again while I painted. I would then paint the sensation as the symbol and use it to guide me to what colors should be part of the symbol. Each alphabet of desire symbol is representative of the experience...but there's a key word to remember.

The symbol is a representation that's meant to help you access the experience at will. The symbol serves as a memory trigger and invocation of the neurotransmitter/bacteria. It helps you call up the experience, at which point the experience takes over and you commune directly with the neurotransmitter/bacteria you've chosen to work with.

You don't need to paint your alphabet of desire symbols, but I recommend fleshing the symbols out further than just a drawing. I found that by doing that it helped me go deeper into the experiences I was having. I recommend creating your own symbols because it will allow you to form a more intimate relationship with the spirits of the body.

Conclusion

With this chapter and the previous two I've shared the basic process for connecting with and starting to work with the neurotransmitters and bacteria in your body. At this point, if this work calls to you, I recommend getting started with creating your own relationships with the neurotransmitters and bacteria of your body. You'll learn a lot from them and begin to discover the true alchemy and mysteries of the body.

In the next two chapters you'll see my alphabet of desire for the neurotransmitters and microbiota as well as my notes on them. In the final two chapters I'll share some experiences and ideas about how you can apply this work to your life.

Chapter 4: Neurotransmitters

In this chapter I'm going to introduce you to the neurotransmitters and amino acids you can work with. I want to note that what I'm sharing is not necessarily an exhaustive list of these entities, but it is fairly extensive. More importantly, if you decide to pursue this work yourself what I share here and in the rest of the book will provide you a jumping off point. I've opted not to include a table of correspondences because part of doing this work involves developing your own correspondences and I don't want to influence that work with my own. However, I am including a high level overview of what the different neurotransmitters affect, which you can use to direct your efforts.

Before I start introducing you to the spirits of the body I want to note two very important details. First, the format of this chapter is a bit different. In each entry I introduce the neurotransmitter and tell you a bit about my own impressions, as well as what the function of the given spirit is when it comes to the body. I also share the painting I created through my meditations.

Second, what I'm sharing with you is essentially my alphabet of desire. While you can use it, I'd strongly urge you to create your own relationships and form your own symbols, because I think you will get a lot more out of the process I shared in previous chapters than just simply using what I'm providing here. The main reason I'm providing these entries is to serve as examples and give you a leg up in your own research and work.

Also, please remember that every spirit I'm describing here is naturally produced by your body and can be worked without having to ingest foreign substances. In fact, I recommend you approach the work this way so you can actually feel how the neurotransmitters and microbiota show up in your body naturally.

With all that said, let me introduce you to the spirits of your body.

Overview of the Neurotransmitters

This overview is based on functionality, specifically what functionality the neurotransmitter affects for the body. The categories are general, and as such you might find that you would create further distinctions. I've mainly provided them as a general overview and a place for you to start in terms of categorizing and organizing how you might work with these spirits.

Mental Health/Neurobiology – Acetylcholine, Asparagine, Aspartate, Dynorphin, Glutamate, Glycine, Hypocretin, Norepinephrine, Serotonin, Serine, Somatostatin, Threonine, Tryptophan, Tyrosine.

Physical Fitness – Acetylcholine, Alanine, GABA, Neurokinin A, Phenethylamine, Testosterone.

Digestion – Biotin, Bombesin, Cholecystokinin, Cortisol, Dynorphin, Gastrin, Ghrelin, Glutamate, Glycine, Hypocretin, Insulin, Isoleucine, Leptin, Motilin, Secretin, Serotonin, Valine.

Waste – Alanine, Aldosterone, Gastrin, Glutamine, Vasopressin.

Immune System/Health – Aldosterone, Arginine, Cortisol, Cysteine, Enkephalin, Estrogen, Glucagon, Glutamate, Glycine, Histamine, Histidine, Insulin, Kisspeptin, Lysine, Melatonin, Methionine, Niacin, Norepinephrine, Secretin, Selenocysteine, Serine, Somatostatin, Substance P, Testosterone, Tyrosine.

DNA/RNA – Adenine, Thymine, Guanine, Cytosine, Uracil.

Pain Management – Anandamide, Betalipotropin, Cortisol, Endorphins, Epinephrine, Neurokinin A, Norepinephrine.

Anxiety/ Stress Management – Corticotrophin, Dynorphin, Endorphins, Epinephrine, GABA, Norepinephrine, Oxytocin, Proline, Serotonin, Tyrosine.

Meditation – Anandamide, Betalipotropin, DMT, Dopamine, Endorphins.

Pleasure – Dopamine, DMT, Endorphins, Estrogen, Gonadotropin, Hypocretin, Kisspeptin, Neurokinin B, Oxytocin, Phenethylamine, Testosterone, Vasopressin.

Acetylcholine

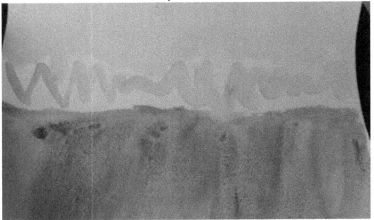

Acetylcholine's anthropomorphic appearance, for me, is a young person who's freshly done with exercising. Non-anthropomorphically, Acetylcholine feels likes movement and connection wrapped up in one. Acetylcholine is helpful with kinesthetic awareness and moving the muscles.

Acetylcholine's function in the brain is to help with arousal, memory, attention and motivation. In the body, Acetylcholine activates the movement of muscles.

I've worked with Acetylcholine to help me enhance my muscle memory and improve my reaction time, as well as just help me age gracefully. I recommend working with it as a way of helping you connect more deeply with your body.

Adenine

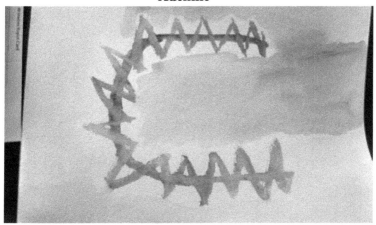

Adenine is one of the 5 elemental protein strands of DNA/RNA. Anthropomorphically Adenine always presents itself to me as a hermaphroditic person. Non-anthropomorphically, Adenine feels like a strand/rung that connects everything together at a primal level.

Adenine meshes with Thymine in DNA and Uracil in RNA. Its primary function is to be a building block of life.

When I've worked with Adenine, I've always worked with it as part of a whole in relationship with the other DNA strands. In appendix 1, I share some of my workings with the 5 elemental proteins.

Alanine

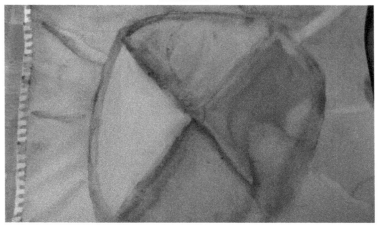

Alanine is an Amino Acid. Anthropomorphically Alanine shows up as a great maned lion. Non-anthropomorphically, Alanine feels like a centering and synthesis of different resources, a cauldron that brings things together. It balances everything and makes sure to remove impurities so the body can become stronger.

Alanine can be created by the body. Alanine works with Glucose to move resources from the muscles of the body to the liver, where they are then purified and brought back to the muscles.

I've worked with Alanine (in conjunction with Glucose) after a good workout, to help with the efficient processing and purification of resources so the muscles can strengthened and toned.

Aldosterone

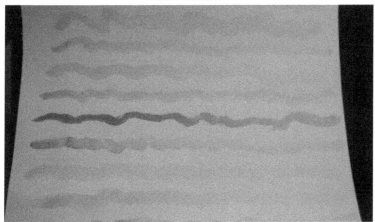

Aldosterone is a steroid hormone. For me, it shows up anthropomorphically as a muscly rat. Non-anthropomorphically it feels like fibrous cords that flex and tighten as needed.

In the body Aldosterone is primarily concerned with conserving sodium in your kidneys, saliva/sweat glands, and the colon. It also plays a role in the regulation of your blood pressure through sodium and potassium.

I've primarily worked with Aldosterone to help with waste processes of the body, while also protecting the organs associated with waste. I've also worked with it to help with controlling blood pressure in stressful situations. I have had it work with Alanine, helping to get rid of the waste and process it efficiently so that the muscles of the body can grow stronger.

Anandamide

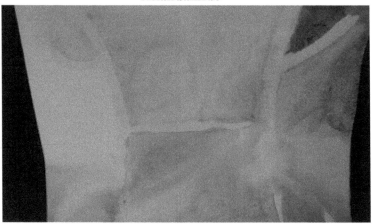

Anandamide is a neurotransmitter. Anthropomorphically anandamide appears to me as a slow slithering snake. Non-anthropomorphically, Anandamide feels like a gentle wave of continual bliss.

In the body Anandamide seems to be a neurotransmitter that generates feelings of pleasure and bliss, as well as enhancement of taste. Anandamide may also have an impairing effect on the memory. I use the word may because this is a recently discovered neurotransmitter.

I've worked with Anandamide primarily in terms of helping to combat pain and provide gentle experiences of pleasure. I've found it quite helpful in terms of generating states of altered consciousness that are conducive to meditation. It can help you achieve a deeper state of altered consciousness. It can also be useful during exercise because it helps you block out pain, while focusing on the benefits of the exercise.

Arginine

Arginine is an amino acid. Anthropomorphically it appears as a set of flexing arms. Non-anthropomorphically it feels like a sensations of muscles flexing and tensing. It's a flowing sensation which never seems to stop.

In the body Arginine is a semi-essential amino acid, which means it may or may not need to be consumed. Arginine helps with healing, cell division, the immune system, and the release of hormones. Arginine can also reduce blood pressure.

My work with Arginine has focused on healing and strengthening the immune system as well as regulating the release of other hormones. I've also found it helpful in stressful situations, where I've used it to reduce my blood pressure.

Asparagine

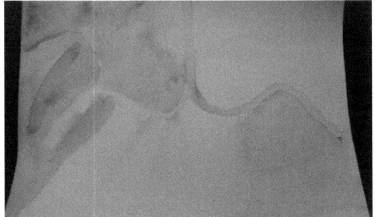

Asparagine is an amino acid used to synthesize proteins. Anthropomorphically Asparagine shows up as a young child with a yo-yo. Non-anthropomorphically it feels like crystalline waves that surge back and forth in the brain, sharpening the connections between thoughts and making sure everything is working the way it's supposed to.

In the body, Asparagine plays a key role in the development and function of the brain.

When I've worked with Asparagine it's been to help enhance the cognitive functions of the brain, making me aware and alert. I've noticed that working with Asparagine regularly has helped my cognitive awareness become sharper and more focused.

Aspartate

Aspartate is a neurotransmitter. Anthropomorphically Aspartate shows up as a stream of liquid. Non-anthropomorphically it feels like a stream of energy that stimulates your brain, sparking connections and keeping the brain active.

As a neurotransmitter, Aspartate helps with memory and with stimulating neural plasticity, which allows the brain to continue adapting and learning.

When I've worked Aspartate I've used it in conjunction with Glutamate to help with neural plasticity and memory retention. My work with Aspartate has helped me in particular with enhancing my memory and being able to create correspondent connections with my memory.

Betalipotropin

Betalipotropin is an amino acid that helps with the creation of neurotransmitters. Anthropomorphically it shows up as a white snake. Non-anthropomorphically it feels like a series of pulsating waves that spread a feeling of pleasurable numbness throughout your body.

In the brain, Betalipotropin is responsible for helping to create melatonin and endorphins. It also stimulates the pituitary gland.

When I've worked with Betalipotropin I've used it to stimulate the pituitary gland which has helped with achieving altered states of consciousness. I've been able to create deeper states of meditation as a result. There is some feeling of numbness that can occur when working with this neurotransmitter.

Biotin

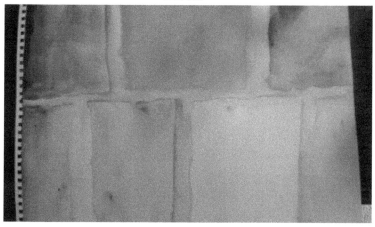

Biotin is a neurotransmitter. Anthropomorphically Biotin appears to me as a wall. Non-anthropomorphically, Biotin feels like a well-ordered sequence that makes order of the things it's supposed to take care of.

Biotin's role in the body is to help with cell growth and the metabolism of amino acids and fats, as well as producing fatty acids. With metabolic activities, Biotin helps with the conversion of carbon dioxide. Biotin can also help with the stability of your blood sugar level.

I've worked with Biotin to help me with metabolism and blood sugar levels. In particular Biotin has been helpful improving the metabolic processes of my body and helping me move from a pre-diabetic state to a normal state of health.

Bombesin

Bombesin is an amino acid. Anthropomorphically Bombesin appears to me as a diet instructor trying to keep me on task. Non-anthropomorphically, Bombesin feels like a swirling sensation that can lock down or open up sensations of hunger.

In the body Bombesin can act as an appetite suppressant, signaling when to stop eating. It also stimulates the release of Gastrin. Bombesin can also help you recognize if certain types of cancer are occurring, specifically, small cell carcinoma of lung, gastric cancer, pancreatic cancer and neuroblastoma.

When I worked with Bombesin I asked it to help me become more aware of my appetite and signal me when I should stop eating. It has helped me be more conscious of my eating. I've worked with it in conjunction with Cholecystokinin, which also can be an appetite suppressant.

Cholecystokinin

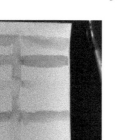

Cholecystokinin is a hormone. Anthropomorphically it appears to me as a pig devouring food. Non-anthropomorphically it feels like the sensation of hunger.

In the body Cholecystokinin shows up in the gastrointestinal system of the body, where it stimulates digestive enzymes and bile which help with the digestion of proteins and fat. It can also act as a hunger suppressant, signaling when to stop eating and inhibiting the release of Gastrin, another hormone. Finally, in the brain, it can cause anxiety.

I've worked with Cholecystokinin to improve the digestion process with meat, while also working in conjunction with Bombesin to signal when I've eaten enough. In the brain I've worked with Cholecystokinin to help me be more aware of anxiety so I can work through it, instead of suppressing it. This has also helped me recognize when I'm eating because of anxiety instead of because of genuine hunger.

Corticotrophin

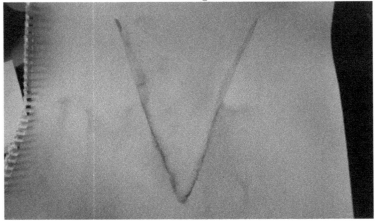

Corticotrophin is a hormone. Anthropomorphically Corticotrophin appears to me as a yellow and blue snake. Non-anthropomorphically Corticotrophin feels like a sharp stabbing awareness that keeps a person on edge.

In the body Corticotrophin is a hormone in the pituitary gland that deals with stress response. It can cause anxiety as well as boost attention. Long-term effects of Corticotrophin can be detrimental, including contributing to general anxiety disorder.

I've worked with Corticotrophin in situations that require focused attention, but I don't recommend long term work because of its link to anxiety. Diminishing its activity can be helpful for limiting anxiety. My work as a result has focused on utilizing Corticotrophin to help with the initial response to a stressful event and then shutting it off after the initial experience.

Cortisol

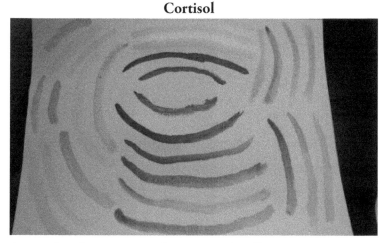

Cortisol is a hormone. Anthropomorphically it appears to me as an exercising person lifting weights. Non-anthropomorphically it feels like the tension and ripping of muscles in the body.

In the body Cortisol is a steroid hormone that is released from the adrenal gland, when a person experiences stress and low blood sugar. It can help increase blood sugar, as well suppress the immune system, which can prevent inflammation. Cortisol also helps with the metabolism of fat, protein and carbohydrates. Cortisol also plays a role in the diurnal cycle of humans and can increase feelings of depression and anxiety. It can enhance short term memory but impair long term memory. Cortisol should be worked with carefully because it can have negative effects on your immune systems and bones.

My work with Cortisol has been a delicate balancing act. Knowing when or when not to employ Cortisol is important. For example, when I recently injured my foot I had Cortisol at work initially to decrease inflammation, but once healing started, I stopped working with Cortisol. My work with Cortisol has always been done in terms of helping with short-term effects, such as dealing with inflammation or mitigating low blood sugar until I could eat.

Cysteine

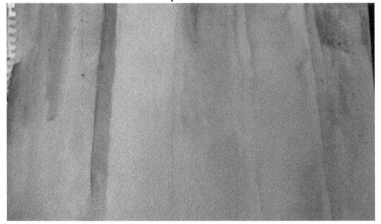

Cysteine is an amino acid. Anthropomorphically Cysteine appears as strands of hair. Non-anthropomorphically Cysteine feels like lines of power that weave through the body.

In the body Cysteine can help reduce the toxic effects of alcohol on the system. It's not an amino acid the body produces so its effect is primarily artificial.

I've worked with Cysteine to counteract the toxic effects of alcohol, but also to improve the overall health of my body.

Cytosine

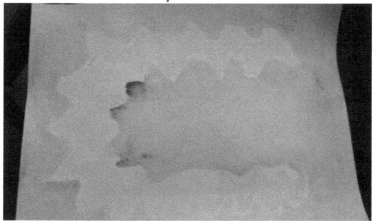

Cytosine is one of the five elements of DNA. Anthropomorphically Cytosine presents itself as a hermaphroditic being. Non-anthropomorphically Cytosine feels like a strand/rung that connects everything together at a primal level.

Cytosine meshes with Guanine in DNA and Uracil in RNA. Its primary function is to be a building block of life. When I've worked with Cytosine, I've always worked with it as part of a whole, along with the rest of the DNA. In appendix 1, I share some of my workings with the 5 elemental proteins.

DMT

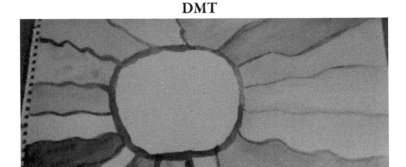

DMT is a neurotransmitter in the brain. Anthropomorphically it shows up as a shining man, and non-anthropomorphically it heightens every sensation and provides visual and audible hallucinations.

DMT does occur naturally in the body, in the cerebro-spinal fluid and pineal gland. It is thought to play a role in our ability to dream. It can also be ingested or inhaled orally (and in such cases is usually done as a way to induce an altered state of consciousness).

I connected with DMT through my pineal gland. When I did I had a very intense experience that last for about an hour, similar to what happens when you ingest DMT. I found that my senses were greatly enhanced and that I experienced a heightened form of Synesthesia, which makes me think that DMT may a play a role in Synesthesia. I wouldn't normally recommend working with DMT through your body on a regular basis unless you're doing a ritual and want to create a heightened state of altered experience You can stress your natural rhythms if you tinker too much with something that plays a role in your dreaming and enhanced states.

Dopamine

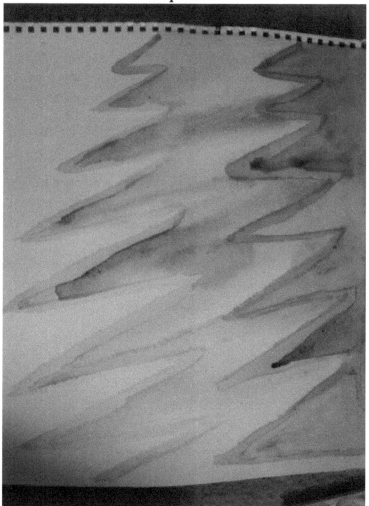

Dopamine always appears to me anthropomorphically as an old trickster, crafty and wise, but you never know what you'll get. When working with Dopamine non-anthropomorphically, it manifests as a tingling, spiking sensation of pleasure that could make you feel really high. Whenever I've worked with Dopamine it's shown up in the form of pleasure, but it also shows up whenever I'm learning something new that I feel very interested in. It essentially rewards the learning experience.

Dopamine's primary function in the brain is to be a reward neurotransmitter, and this comes into play whether you're doing activities or taking entheogen substances (and in this capacity can be addictive). Dopamine also plays a role in motor functions and the controlled release of hormones in the body.

In the body Dopamine performs specific functions. With blood vessels it inhibits the release of Norepinephrine and widens the blood vessels. In the kidneys it increases urination and sodium excretion, while in the pancreas it reduces insulin production. In the intestines it stimulates the mucus that protects the intestine. In the immune system, it reduces the activity of lymphocytes.

While you can work with Dopamine to stimulate pleasure, I recommend not overdoing it. Instead I'd suggest focusing on using Dopamine to help you with the regulation of your body and to stimulate interest in what you're learning.

Dynorphin

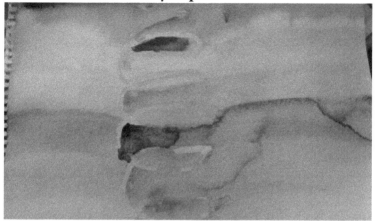

Dynorphin are opoid peptides. Anthropomorphically Dynorphin appears as a 6 armed, 3 faced deity. Non-anthropomorphically, Dynorphin feels like a mutating, changing spiral.

In the body Dynorphin actually has three different variations, Dynorphin A, B, and Big. Each version contains amino acid residue. Dynorphins are found in the spinal cord and brain. Dynorphin performs a variety of functions in the brain, which can include affecting the control of appetite and pain and body temperature, suppressing neurotransmitters, and even playing a role in the patterning of electrical activity in the brain. Suppressing Dynorphin can help with depression and addition behaviors.

Because Dynorphin performs a variety of functions, I recommend spending some extended time getting to know Dynorphin and figuring out when to employ it and when to suppress it. I've found Dynorphin helpful in mapping out the electrical patterns of the brain and in maintaining a careful balance with the functions it can control.

Endorphins

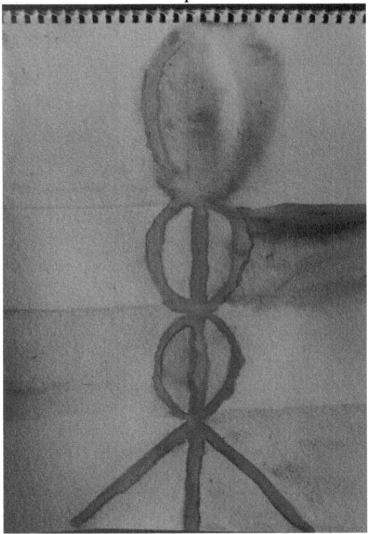

Endorphins are neuropeptides and hormones. Anthropomorphically, Endorphins shows up to me as a runner. Non-anthropomorphically I feel a deep sense of pleasure and satisfaction that ripples through my body.

In the body Endorphins show up in the pituitary gland and the central nervous system. They can help with inhibiting pain while also enhancing pleasure. In my work with Endorphins I've used them to help inhibit feelings of pain as well as enhance feelings of pleasure, particularly around exercise, which in turn has helped make it easier to want to exercise. They also enhance sexual and sensual pleasure and when worked with and can play a role in higher libido.

Enkephalin

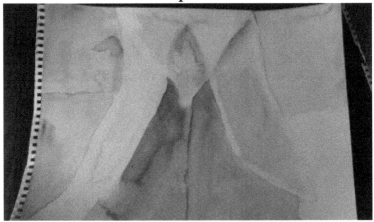

Enkephalin is a pentapeptide. It appears to me anthropomorphically as a noxious gas. Non-anthropomorphically it shows up as a feeling of nausea.

In the body Enkephalin is responsible for controlling the body's reaction to stimuli that are harmful to it. For example, when you cry while cutting onions that would be a stimuli reacting to something harmful (the smell/fumes of the onion). My work with Enkephalin has involved fine tuning what it does to make my body aware of such stimuli. Beyond that I don't recommend inhibiting it because it performs a valuable service by making you aware of something that could be harmful to you.

Epinephrine (aka Adrenalin)

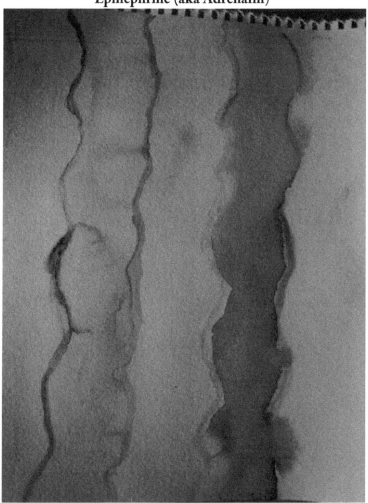

Epinephrine, also known as Adrenalin, is a hormone and neurotransmitter. Anthropomorphically, Epinephrine shows up as a yellow snake. Non-anthropomorphically, Epinephrine feels like a burning, rushing sensation that simultaneously empowers you and drains you.

In the body, Epinephrine is produced by the adrenal glands. Epinephrine is activated in any fight or flight or survival situation. It also shows up when a person is engaged in exercise or any other activity that involves physical exertion, but can also be activated by emotions, particularly anger, rage, fear, and hatred. Under certain circumstances Epinephrine can also enhance memories, usually traumatic ones.

I recommend working with Epinephrine sparingly, because it can be burn you out while you become more reliant upon it. My work with Epinephrine has mostly been focused around improving reflexes in stressful situations.

Estrogen

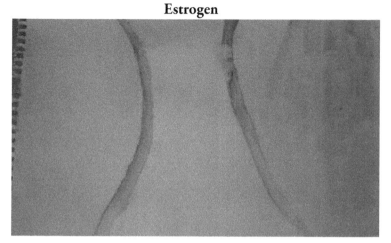

Estrogen is a hormone. Anthropomorphically it shows up as a young woman. Non-anthropomorphically Estrogen feels like an expansion and contraction of energy all at the same time.

In the body Estrogen develops and regulates the female reproductive system, but also plays a role in other sexual aspects in both biological sexes. Estrogen performs a variety of other activities that can help the body in various ways, including helping with breathing, appetite suppression, and even the handling of bodily waste.

Estrogen has helped me with my sex drive, as well as handling the various activities for the body that it influences. I haven't done much to change it because it seems to work just fine as is, but if you don't have enough Estrogen it can be very helpful to create a relationship that makes Estrogen your ally. For women, working with Estrogen can also be helpful if you want to get pregnant.

GABA

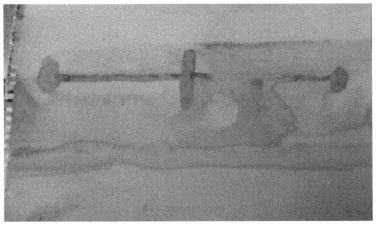

GABA is a neurotransmitter. Anthropomorphically GABA shows up as a constriction band that is being tensed. Non-anthropomorphically GABA feels like a smooth sensation that is getting ridding of imperfections, while strengthening what is being toned.

In the body, GABA is responsible for toning the muscles of the body. It also reduces the neuronal excitation in the brain.

In my work with GABA I've used it to help with the suppression of certain states of mind such as depression and anxiety. I've also worked with GABA to improve my muscle tone and help me increase my physical strength. When I work with GABA I feel this sense of equilibrium and evening out which helps to keep matters in perspective.

Gastrin

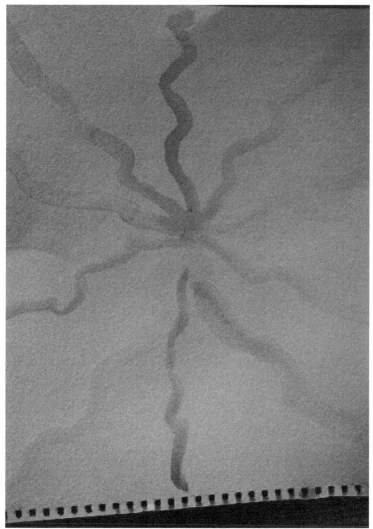

Gastrin is a hormone. Anthropomorphically it appears to me as a hungry person, looking for food. Non-anthropomorphically it feels like saliva being generated when you feel hungry.

In the body Gastrin is responsible for stimulating the digestion and waste processes of the body. When activated Gastrin stimulates the production of stomach acids in the stomach, while also stimulating the pancreas and gall bladder to start waste removal.

My work with Gastrin has primarily focused on learning more about digestive and waste production of my body, so I can improve what I'm eating. I've also worked with Gastrin to improve the processing of food into waste. This work has changed some of my diet as a result so that I eat less meat, as Gastrin suggested a diet change to improve my digestion.

Ghrelin

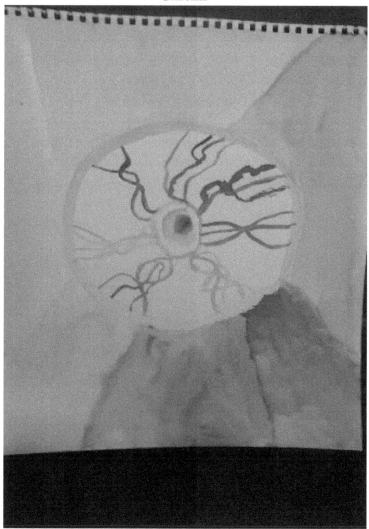

Ghrelin is a hormone. Anthropomorphically it appears to me as a salivating mouth. Non-anthropomorphically Ghrelin feels like hunger pangs, and the sensation of closing hunger down or opening hunger up to be felt.

In the body, Ghrelin regulates appetite while also playing a central role in the energy homeostasis of the body which is the distribution and rate of use of energy. When your body feels hungry, Ghrelin stimulates the release of Gastrin and gets the intestines ready for digestion. Ghrelin uses the energy levels of the body as well as the body weight etc., to determine when to eat, while also helping with the conversion of food into nutrients and energy.

My work with Ghrelin has focused on fine tuning the energy conversion process involved with eating, while also increasing metabolism in order to help with weight control. At the same time Ghrelin has helped me pay better attention to hunger signals so I eat at the right times to help my energy level.

Glucagon

Glucagon is a hormone. Anthropomorphically it appears to me as a growing boy. Non-anthropomorphically it feels like a sensation of change and growth.

In the body, Glucagon is produced by the pancreas. Its main function is to raise glucose and fat in the bloodstream. It focuses on stabilizing the blood glucose levels and does this in conjunction with insulin, with each balancing the other out. Glucagon can increase the amount of energy expended, and as such shows up in high concentration during stressful situations.

My work with Glucagon has been done in conjunction with insulin to further stabilize my blood glucose levels and to enhance my natural stamina. As a result, so that if I can't get nutrients right away, I can still function until I have access to nutrients that would help with the blood glucose levels.

Glutamine

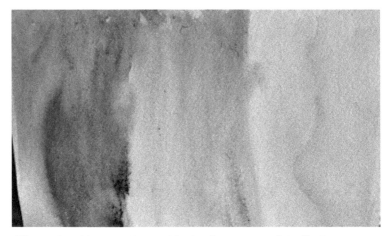

Glutamine is an amino acid. Anthropomorphically it appears as a scale. Non-anthropomorphically it feels like a sense of balance and weights.

In the body, Glutamine is responsible for the synthesis of proteins and lipids. It also regulates and transports ammonium in the body and helps with the production of energy in the cells.

My work with Glutamine has been focused on working with its production of cellular energy, while also regulating waste. At the same time, I've carefully worked with Glutamine to target what it feeds and helps in the body, since it can sometimes be a source of nutrients for cancer cells, and as such I've made it a point to redirect it from any such potential cells.

Glutamate

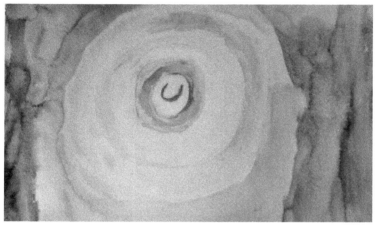

Glutamate is a neurotransmitter. Anthropomorphically it appears as a devouring mouth. Non-anthropomorphically the sensation is a feeling of constant change that produces energy.

In the body Glutamate plays a central role in cellular metabolism by breaking down proteins and turning them into energy for the cells. Glutamate is also the most abundant neurotransmitter in the brain, where it plays a significant role in our ability to learn and memory while also strengthening the connection between synapses in the brain.

My work with Glutamate has focused on both regulating the metabolism of my body and improving my ability to learn and memorize. When I worked with it I found my learning and memorization improved because of using Glutamate to strengthen the neural connections.

Glycine

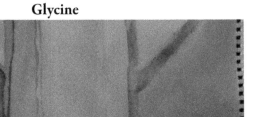

Glycine is a neurotransmitter. Anthropomorphically it shows up as a shield or a stop sign. Non-Anthropomorphically it feels like boundaries and walks that keep everything in their proper place.

In the body, Glycine acts as an inhibitor, balancing Glutamate to make sure that receptors are activated without malfunctioning.

My work with Glycine has focused on matching it with the work I do with Glutamate to make sure everything runs seamlessly.

Gonadotropin

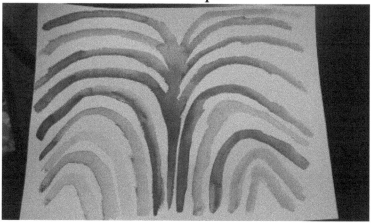

Gonadotropin is a hormone. Anthropomorphically it shows up as a blooming flower. Non-anthropomorphically it feels like an orgasmic burst of pleasure.

In the body Gonadotropin regulates sexual development and reproduction.

My work with Gonadotropin has focused around increasing or decreasing sexual hormones as needed. I find that it's useful to work with this hormone if you need help with regulating your sex drive, either to make it more or less active.

Guanine

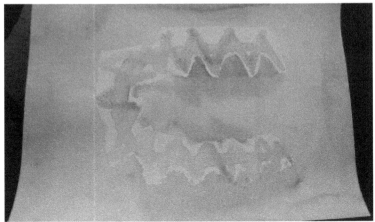

Guanine is one of the five elements of DNA. Anthropomorphically Guanine presents itself as a hermaphroditic being. Non-anthropomorphically, Guanine always feels like a strand/rung that connects everything together at a primal level.

Guanine meshes with Cytosine in DNA and Uracil in RNA. Its primary function is to be a building block of life. When I've worked with Guanine, I've always worked with it as part of a whole, along with the rest of the DNA. In appendix 1, I share some of my workings with the 5 elemental proteins.

Histamine

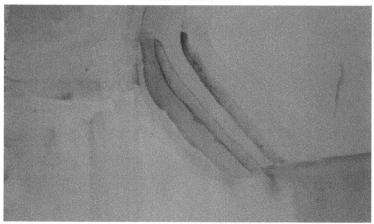

Histamine is a neurotransmitter. Anthropomorphically it shows up as an itching man. Non-anthropomorphically it feels like an itch.

In the body, Histamine plays a role in immune responses, particularly making your aware of allergic reactions, as well as helping to fight infections. Histamine also helps to regulate the gut. Histamine can also be used to lower blood pressure. Histamine can also cause wakefulness and prevent sleep.

My work with Histamine has mostly involved strengthening my immune system response, and in certain situations inducing wakefulness, such as when feeling tired at work, but needing to be awake.

Histidine

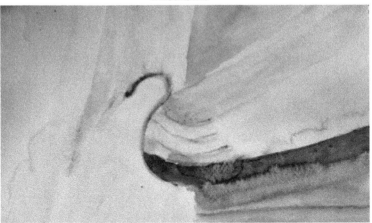

Histidine is an amino acid. Anthropomorphically it appears as bird. Non-anthropomorphically it feels like a spiral.

In the body Histidine must be consumed and plays a necessary role in producing Histamine, as well as helping with growth and development of the body's response to Histamine

My work with Histidine has focused on improving the synthesis of Histamine and helping the development of the body's response, but also setting it up so that I can regulate that response.

Hypocretin

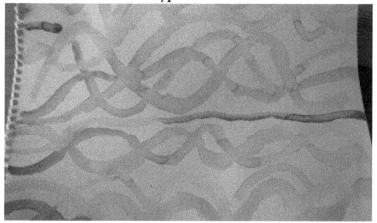

Hypocretin is a neurotransmitter. Anthropomorphically it appears as multi-limbed person, performing multiple functions. Non-anthropomorphically it feels like a network that's running through your body.

In the body, Hypocretin helps with the regulation of arousal, wakefulness, and appetite. Hypocretin helps determine how awake a person should be. Hypocretin also affects appetite by suppressing inhibitory digestive feedback, making it possible to overeat. In fact, Hypocretin can induce overeating if a person is not getting enough sleep. Hypocretin can suppress addiction to alcohol, smoking, and other substances. If a person has a lot of Hypocretin it can make them happier, and if not as much it can make them feel depressed.

I've worked with Hypocretin to induce deeper more restful sleep, which has helped cut down on appetite and also increased a general sense of happiness in my life. At the same time I've also worked with Hypocretin to help me be more awake when I need to be.

Insulin

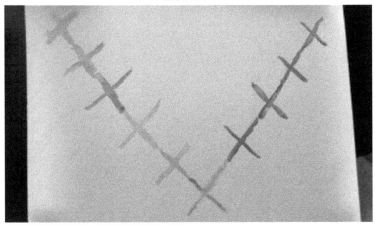

Insulin is a hormone. Anthropomorphically it appears as a marching soldier. Non-anthropomorphically it feels like a mesh that fits through the body.

In the body Insulin regulates the metabolism of carbohydrates, fats, and proteins through the absorption of glucose. Insulin helps with the conversion of proteins in different organs. Insulin also helps with cognition, learning, and memorization.

My work with Insulin has involved Insulin encouraging me to make activity and diet changes, which have enhanced my life and learning and improved my overall health. I feel Insulin move through me and check to make sure everything is working right and in a balanced manner.

Isoleucine

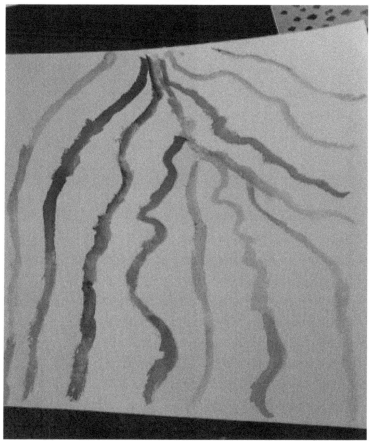

Isoleucine is an amino acid. Anthropomorphically it appears as a young doctor. Non-anthropomorphically it feels like branches that go through the mesh of Insulin and contain it.

In the body Isoleucine can raise blood glucose levels. It's an essential amino acid that needs to be digested. My work with Isoleucine has mainly been done in conjunction with lowering blood glucose levels, while also getting essential nutrients from it.

Kisspeptin

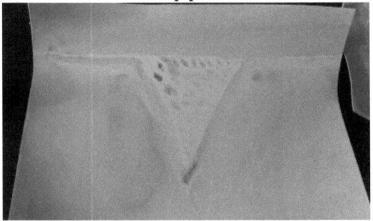

Kisspeptin is a protein. Anthropomorphically it appears as a guardian. Non-anthropomorphically it feels like a door that carefully monitors what is allowed through.

In the body Kisspeptin is a protein that can suppress melanoma and breast cancer metastasis. Kisspeptin also stimulates Gonadotropin and Aldosterone, helping with reproduction and adrenaline.

My work with Kisspeptin has been done to help with either stimulating or suppressing Gonadotropin and Aldosterone. I feel like it acts as a gate keeper that regulates the body and keeps it running and healthy.

Leptin

Leptin is a hormone. Anthropomorphically it appears as a doorkeeper. Non-anthropomorphically it feels like fullness, after you've eaten a good meal.

In the body Leptin is responsible for suppressing hunger and counteracting Ghrelin. It signals when to stop eating.

I've worked with Leptin to help regulate my appetite and insure I don't eat too much. This work has been particularly helpful with exercise, because I'll raise Leptin levels after exercising to ensure portion control.

Leucine

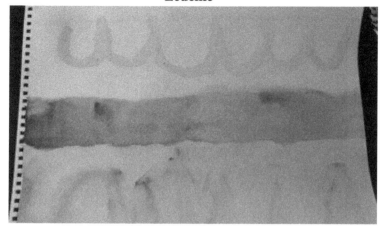

Leucine is an amino acid. Anthropomorphically it appears as a cloudy haze that surrounds you. Non-anthropomorphically it feels like the ache in your muscles after a good work out.

In the body Leucine stimulates the protein for muscles in order to slow the atrophying of muscles or to help the muscles adjust to becoming stronger as a result of exercise.

I've worked with Leucine to help my muscles recover faster from workouts. Stimulating Leucine helps produce more protein and process that protein to help your body heal from the workout and get stronger.

Lysine

Lysine is an amino acid. Anthropomorphically it appears as a walking suit of skin. Non-anthropomorphically it feels like the sensation of air on skin.

In the body Lysine is an essential amino acid. Lysine helps with your skin and can help with the healing of wounds on the skin as well as the health of the skin.

My work with Lysine has focused on improving the health of my skin, as well as its ability to heal.

Melatonin

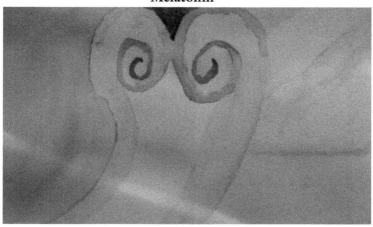

Melatonin is a hormone. Anthropomorphically it appears as a woman with black hair and skin. Non-anthropomorphically it is the feeling that occurs when you are tired and should go to sleep. It feels like you need to yawn.

Melatonin helps to regulate the sleep cycle of the body through the entrainment of the circadian rhythms of the body. Melatonin also acts an antioxidant for the body, which can be helpful in counteracting cancer.

I've primarily worked with Melatonin to help myself go to sleep, but I've also worked with it to help purify and cleanse my body. It helps a lot when I'm struggling to sleep because it can counteract the feeling of insomnia.

Methionine

Methionine is an amino acid. Anthropomorphically it appears as a stream of blood. Non-anthropomorphically it feels like a sensation of growth and division.

In the body, Methionine aids in the growth of blood vessels.

My work with Methionine has been focused on regulating it as too much of it can lead to cancer. Beyond that I've simply let it do what it needs to do.

Motilin

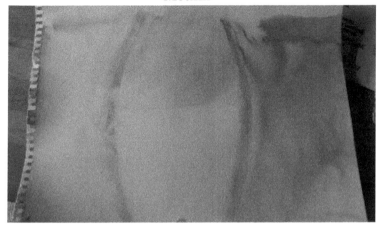

Motilin is an amino acid. Anthropomorphically Motilin appears as an expanding and contracting bubble. Non-anthropomorphically Motilin feels like contractions that tense and ease.

In the body, Motilin controls the contractions of the body the migrate food through the digestive tract. It keeps the digestion on a schedule and moves the meals in the gut to the next destination to make way for the next meal.

My work with Motilin has focused on simply being aware of the contractions with my body awareness and, on occasion, helping encourage the digestion of food.

Neurokinin A

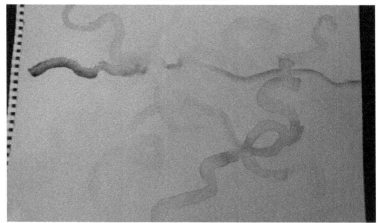

Neurokinin A is a neurotransmitter. Anthropomorphically it appears as fibers that flex. Non-anthropomorphically it feels like the sensation of strength in your muscles.

In the body Neurokinin A helps with muscle contractions, as well as helping your body respond to harmful stimuli. Neurokinin A plays a role in the body's reaction to pain and inflammation. High levels of Neurokinin A can be an indicator of fibromyalgia and epilepsy and have some effect on mood.

My work with Neurokinin A has focused on helping with muscle contractions during exercises and otherwise keeping it at manageable, healthy levels in my body.

Neurokinin B

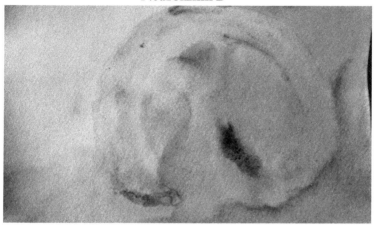

Neurokinin B is a neurotransmitter. Anthropomorphically it appears as a person pleasuring themselves sexually. Non-anthropomorphically it feels like the desire a person feels in their genitals when they want sex.

In the body Neurokinin B plays a significant role in sexual activity and in pregnancy for women. Neurokinin B also stimulates the release of Gonadotropin. Typically Neurokinin B is much more prevalent in women, but there is also some in men.

My work with Neurokinin B has focused on adjusting the sexual drive, either by making it more excited or quieter as needed.

Niacin

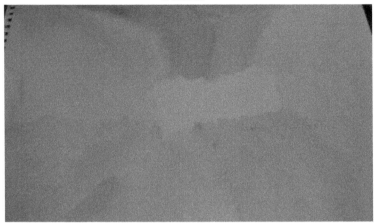

Niacin is an organic compound. Anthropomorphically Niacin appears as a doctor. Non-anthropomorphically Niacin feels like a sensation of blood pressure and panic.

In the body Niacin helps with high blood cholesterol and prevents the disease pellagra, as well as aiding in digestion.

My work with Niacin has focused on using it to help with blood pressure and cholesterol, specifically in regulating my blood pressure and making sure the cholesterol levels are healthy. I've also worked with it to help my digestion.

Norepinephrine

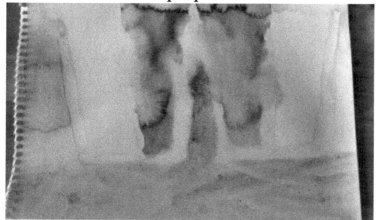

Norepinephrine is a neurotransmitter. Anthropomorphically it appears as a person running. Non-anthropomorphically it feels like a sensation of activity rippling through the body.

In the body Norepinephrine is responsible for the action of the brain and body. When released into the body it makes organs function better for activity by stimulating necessary physiological responses (such as causing the eyes to moisten when using them). Norepinephrine helps with states of arousal and stress response, as well as recalling memories and focusing attention. It can increase anxiety and raise blood pressure.

My work with Norepinephrine has involved streamlining what it does to the body to enhance activity and wakefulness, while also decreasing negative effects such as anxiety.

Oxytocin

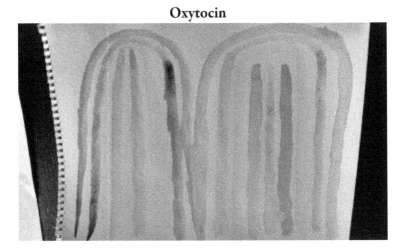

Oxytocin is a hormone. Anthropomorphically it appears as a cuddling couple. Non-anthropomorphically it feels like a warm sensation of merging and closeness.

In the body Oxytocin helps people bond socially and sexually. Oxytocin is also responsible for helping new mothers bond with the baby when the baby is born. Oxytocin can also control feelings of anxiety, fear, and depression.

My work with Oxytocin has involved learning how to connect with other people better and to help in the process of opening up and expressing feelings with my partner. It's also involved using that bonding feeling to bring comfort to myself during stressful moments.

Phenethylamine

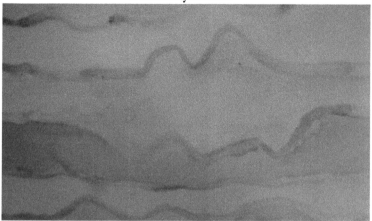

Phenethylamine is a neurotransmitter. Anthropomorphically it appears as a bar of chocolate. Non-anthropomorphically it feels like a sugar rush.

Phenethylamine is found lots of food. It is significantly increased in your body if you exercise for at least 30 minutes. It helps produce Norepinephrine and Dopamine. It also helps produce the euphoric feeling of runners high when exercising.

My work with Phenethylamine has focused on using it to induce me to want to continue exercising regularly.

Proline

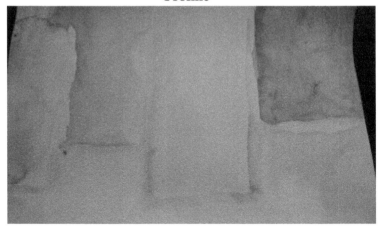

Proline is an amino acid. Anthropomorphically Proline appears as a stressed person. Non-anthropomorphically it feels like a rigid set of uncompromising walls.

In the body Proline play a role in stress responses. Too much of it can have a detrimental effect on the body, damaging never cells.

My work with Proline has focused on keeping it at safe levels, but also using it to help me recognize stress.

Secretin

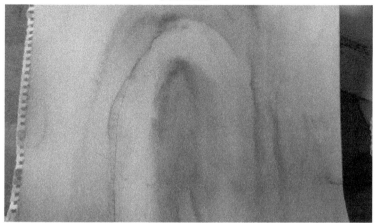

Secretin is a hormone. Anthropomorphically it appears as a river. Non-anthropomorphically it feels like the ebbing and flowing tides of water.

In the body secretin regulates the homeostasis of water in the body, making sure that there is a balance of electrolytes. It also regulates the secretions of the stomach, pancreas and liver.

I've purposely chosen not to work with Secretin, opting to allowing it to do what it usually does, but I do keep an awareness of it so I can adjust and modify if needed.

Selenocysteine

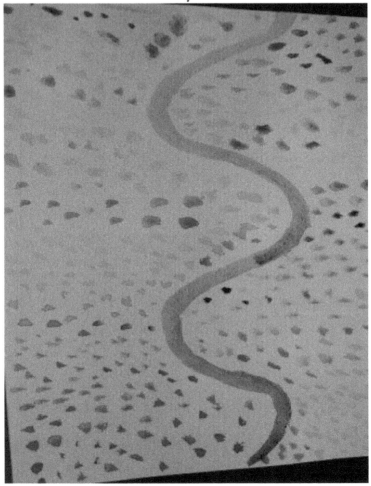

Selenocysteine is an amino acid. Anthropomorphically it appears as a shower of light. Non-anthropomorphically it feels like a wave of energy.

In the body Selenocysteine acts an antioxidant. My work with Selenocysteine has focused on using it to target free radicals, junk DNA which causes cancer, in the body.

Serine

Serine is an amino acid. Anthropomorphically it appears as a junction that connects things together. Non-anthropomorphically it feels like waves of energy which are processed and changed.

In the body Serine helps to metabolize the purines and pyramidines, and is also a precursor to Glycine, Cysteine, and Tryptophan. Serine helps with the catalyzing of enzymes and can additionally signal the activation or repression of other neurotransmitters.

When I've worked with Serine it's basically been like using a switch box to turn on or off other neurotransmitters. I think of it as a junction that helps regulate and choose what's best.

Serotonin

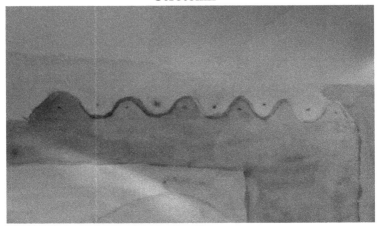

Anthropomorphically, Serotonin appears as a 6 eyed red snake, with three eyes on either side on its face. When working with it non-anthropomorphically Serotonin presents itself as wave of sorts that helps to regulate and stabilize emotions.

I worked with Serotonin when I was 20. At the time I was terribly depressed and had been for years. I didn't want to use medicine because of the side effects, so I developed a meditation that allowed me to go into my body, connect with Serotonin and tweak the re-uptake cycles so Serotonin wasn't absorbed right away. As a result of making that change I was able to get rid of the chemical predisposition to depression and became much happier afterward.

Serotonin regulates moods and can produce states of happiness and well-being. Serotonin also helps with the regulation of appetite and sleep, and can help with memory and learning.

I primarily recommending working with Serotonin to help you with emotional stability, but be careful not to overdo the work. Serotonin will act to make sure you don't go overboard in working with it. You can also work with Serotonin to help you regulate how much you eat.

Somatostatin

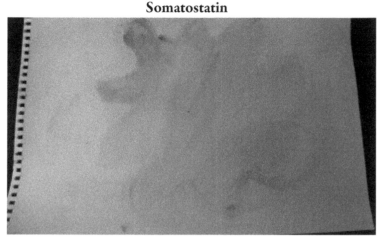

Somatostatin is a hormone. Anthropomorphically it shows up as a child that grows and then stops growing. Non-anthropomorphically it feels like an experience of expansion which then slows down and stops.

In the body, Somatostatin regulates the endocrine system of the body and the proliferation of cells in the body. It can suppress the release of Insulin and Glucagon in the body. Somatostatin also inhibits the release of growth hormone.

My work with Somatostatin has involved collaboration with it on the proliferation of the cells, in order for me to enhance communication with the cells. I've also used Somatostatin to work with the endocrine system in order to more easily connect with neurotransmitters and hormones.

Substance P

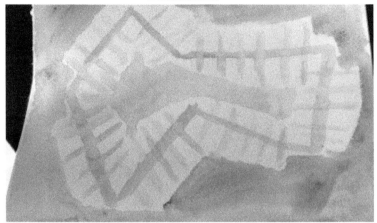

Substance P is a neurotransmitter. Anthropomorphically it appears as a person in pain. Non-anthropomorphically it feels like sharp sensations of pain.

Substance P creates the initial response to stimulus in your environment that is painful or sick. For example, it can cause you to feel nauseous or to vomit. Substance P sends signals for inflammation when you are injured. Substance P can also play a role in helping wounds heal.

My work with Substance P has involved working with it to help me heal wounds quicker as well as helping me beware of anything that could cause me to feel nauseous or sick. I've also used it to help me discover the source of inflammation with some of my joints, which in turn has helped with healing work.

Testosterone

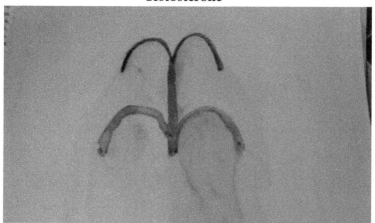

Testosterone is a hormone. Anthropomorphically it appears as a young, arrogant man. Non-anthropomorphically it feels like a feeling of aggression.

In the body, Testosterone plays a significant role in the development of male sexual organs, as well as the development of body hair and muscle mass. Testosterone is also involved in health and well-being, and preventing bone loss.

My own work with Testosterone has involved working with it to increase muscle mass for exercise, as well as for helping with sexual activity.

Threonine

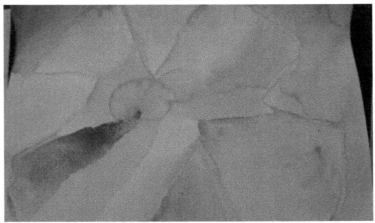

Threonine is an amino acid. Anthropomorphically it appears as a bird. Non-anthropomorphically it feels like a sensation of nutrient, of taking in something you need.

In the body Threonine is an essential amino acid which needs to be eaten each day. It helps to produce Glycine for the brain.

I haven't done any work with Threonine. Its main purpose is to produce Glycine, so it's essential, but beyond that there isn't much it seems to do.

Thymine

Thymine is one of the five elements of DNA. Anthropomorphically Thymine presents itself as a hermaphroditic being. Non-anthropomorphically, Thymine has always felt like a strand/rung that connects everything together at a primal level.

Thymine meshes with Adenine in DNA. In RNA Thymine is replaced by Uracil. Its primary function is to be a building block of life. When I've worked with Thymine I've always worked with it as part of a whole, along with the rest of the DNA. In Appendix 1, I share some of my workings with the 5 elemental proteins.

Tryptophan

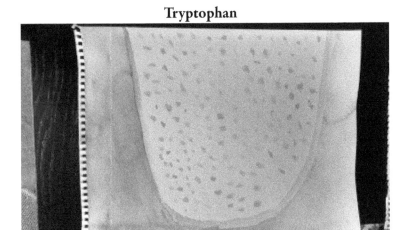

Tryptophan is an amino acid. Anthropomorphically Tryptophan appears in the form of a turkey. Non-anthropomorphically it feels like a sensation of sleepiness.

Tryptophan is an essential amino acid. Tryptophan plays a role in the creation of Serotonin, Melatonin, Niacin, and Auxins.

My work with Tryptophan has involved working with it to produce more Serotonin, Melatonin and Niacin.

Tyrosine

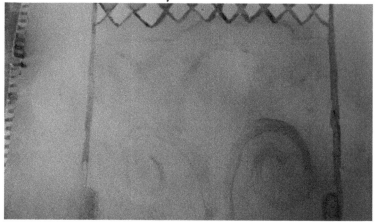

Tyrosine is an amino acid. Anthropomorphically it appears as a radio signal. Non-anthropomorphically it feels like a sensation of transmission.

In the body, Tyrosine helps with signal transmission and helps create Dopamine and Norepinephrine. Tyrosine helps reduce stress hormones and can help with cold, fatigue, and sleep deprivation, as well as improving cognition and physical performance. It can also help with memory during multi-tasking.

My work with Tyrosine has involved it using to help me reduce stress and improve my immune system response to stress and colds. I've also used it to help me during stressful situations with my mind, to keep me sharp.

Uracil

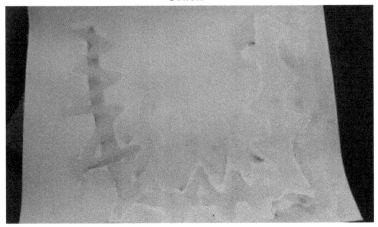

Uracil is one of the five elements of DNA. Anthropomorphically Uracil presents itself as a hermaphroditic being. Non-anthropomorphically, Uracil feels like a strand/rung that connects everything together at a primal level.

Uracil meshes with Adenine, Cytosine, and Guanine in RNA. In DNA Thymine replaces Uracil. Its primary function is to be a building block of life. When I've worked with Uracil, I've always worked with it as part of a whole, along with the rest of the elemental DNA. In Appendix 1, I share some of my workings with the 5 elemental proteins.

Valine

Valine is an amino acid. Anthropomorphically it appears as a shield. Non-anthropomorphically it feels like a sensation of blocking or resistance.

In the body, Valine resists Insulin. It's an essential amino acid, which means we have to have it in our diet, but it's important to maintain a careful balance.

My work with Valine has involved making sure there isn't too much of it because of how it can raise blood glucose levels. I make sure there is some of it, but not too much so that Insulin can do its work.

Vasopressin

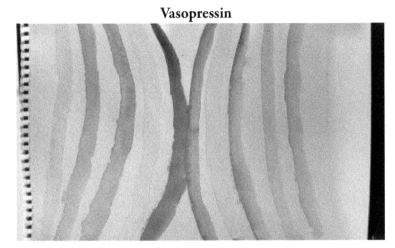

Vasopressin is a hormone. Anthropomorphically Vasopressin shows up a stream of water. Non-anthropomorphically it feels like the sensation of peeing.

In the body, Vasopressin maintains the balance of fluids in the body, making sure they stay separate from each other. Vasopressin makes Kidney's reabsorb water that is toxin free, while also making sure urination happens. Vasopressin increases the absorption of Sodium. Vasopressin can also have an effect on the sex drive.

I've worked with Vasopressin to help improve the process of bodily waste and to help with sexual fluids.

Chapter 5 Archaea, Bacteria, Protozoa

In this chapter, I'm going to introduce you to the microbiota of the body, as well as Mucus. Each of these are distinct life forms, other than Mucus. Each of them, including Mucus, performs specific functions in your body that usually help you maintain your health, but under the wrong circumstances can cause health issues for you.

It's important to become allies with microbiota in your body because by working with them as allies you will find that they take care of you in ways you would never expect. They can teach you how to connect more closely with the rhythms of your body, and at the same time make you aware of just how interconnected your life is with the life that exists in and on you.

Archaea

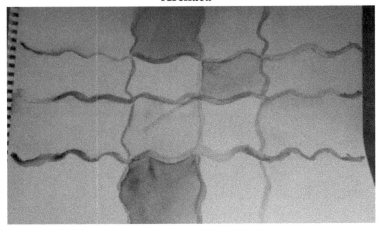

Archaea are Prokaryote microbes. They have no cell nucleus or membrane bound organelles. Anthropomorphically they show up as centipedes to me. Non-anthropomorphically they've felt like a mass of wet, moist movement which is all moving toward the same goal. They are endlessly replicating and endlessly consuming and endlessly excreting.

In the body, Archaea can be found in the colon and digestive tracts, as well as oral cavities and on the skin. They help us digest food and process waste. They also can have an influence on the calorie harvest and body fat of a person. Too much of them can make us obese, especially if the wrong types of food are consumed.

I've worked with Archaea to improve the waste processing and digestion of my body, and it's what I'd recommend if you were to try and work with Archaea. In my work with them I've been able to fine tune my diet so there aren't too many of them, while also working with them to help me keep my body healthy.

Mucus

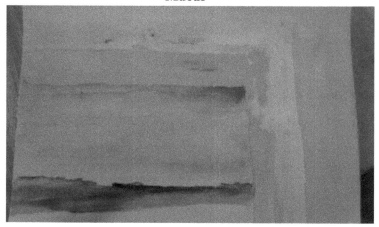

Mucus is a liquid secretion of the body. Anthropomorphically it shows up as a vaguely human form of sticky liquid. Non-anthropomorphically it feels like a thick liquid that flows around and protects the body.

In the body Mucus is used in the nasal passage to protect the lungs and respiratory system from the particles that are inhaled in the air. In the stomach Mucus is used to aid in digestion, and in the genital region Mucus is used to help with the passing of waste.

My work with Mucus has focused on working with it to help me be aware of possible sickness so I can take a proactive approach to fighting off the illness. By paying attention to the amount of Mucus that is being secreted, specifically if more is being secreted than normal, I'm able to take actions such as getting more sleep and getting the Mucus out of my body so I can get back to a better state of health.

Protozoa

Protozoa are single celled. Anthropomorphically they appear as a single cell with flagella. Non-anthropomorphically they feel like a stacked set of cells in the body.

Protozoa have animal behavior such as motility (the ability to move) and predation (meaning they are predators). In the human body they function either as symbionts, living in symbiosis with us or as parasites causing infections.

My work with Protozoa has focused on working with the symbiotic aspect of Protozoa and to aid in digestion and waste removal.

Skin Bacteria (flora)

Skin Bacteria is bacteria on the skin that either isn't harmful to the body or provides a beneficial effect to the body. Anthropomorphically it appears in the shape of a human figure of skin. Non-anthropomorphically it feels like the subtle sensations a person experiences on their skin.

In the body skin bacteria protect the body by getting rid of foreign bacteria. However skin bacteria can also be potentially harmful if a person has a weakened immune system or damaged skin tissue. For example, staph infections are caused by staph bacteria on the skin that while normally helpful, can cause infection when there is damage to the skin. Acne is also caused by skin bacteria.

My work with skin bacteria has focused on allowing it to perform its beneficial functions, while also making sure it doesn't cause infections. Mainly I just monitor it.

Skin Fungus

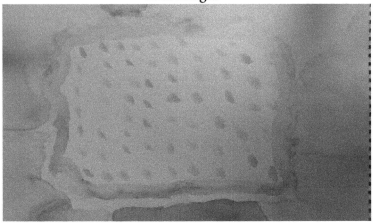

Skin Fungus is fungus that is on the surface of the body. Anthropomorphically it appears as white spores. Non-anthropomorphically its feels like the itchy sensation on skin.

Much like skin bacteria, Skin Fungus can be either beneficial or harmful. It can protect the body from foreign organisms, but too much of it can cause skin infections such as Athletes' Foot.

My work with Skin Fungus has focused on allowing it to perform its beneficial functions, while also making sure it doesn't cause infections. Mainly I just monitor it.

Stomach Bacteria

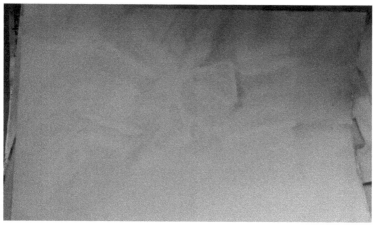

Stomach Bacteria is part of the gut flora in the body. Anthropomorphically it appears as a teeming horde of small creatures. Non-anthropomorphically it feels like the sensation of being full.

In the body, Stomach Bacteria provides a helpful function. We actually need Stomach Bacteria in order to digest and process food. Stomach Bacteria help with the immune system, processing of waste, and the production of vitamins, as well as specific hormones that help store fat. However, Stomach Bacteria can also play a role in obesity and can also cause infections via ulcers. Additionally, they can increase the risk of cancer.

My work with Stomach Bacteria has focused on allowing it to perform its beneficial functions, while making sure it doesn't cause infections. I have also worked to maintain a careful balance of the bacteria, to help with digestion, but not cause obesity.

Stomach Fungus

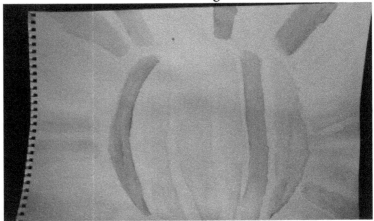

Stomach Fungus is fungus that is found in the gut of the human body.   Anthropomorphically   it   appears   as   yeast. Non-anthropomorphically it feels like a sensation of growth in the stomach.

In the body Stomach Fungus helps with the process of digestion, but like Stomach Bacteria can also have detrimental effects, playing a role in irritable bowel syndrome as well as Hepatitis B.

My work with Stomach Fungus has focused on allowing it to perform its beneficial functions while also making sure it doesn't cause infections or irritation. Mainly I just monitor it.

Chapter 6: Advanced Work with the Biology of the Body

Now that we've done the connection work with the neurotransmitters and microbiota of the body, we need to start exploring what we can do with those connections and how we can improve the health the body as a result. It's also important to note that just because you can work with a neurotransmitter or bacteria doesn't mean you have to. Ideally, if you've done the connection work and not just read what I shared previously, you'll have a feeling for how a given neurotransmitter or microbiota works and you'll be able to determine whether you should work with it, or just monitor it and let it do what it needs to do.

I'm going to break this chapter down into two segments. The first segment explores working with one given neurotransmitter or microbiota. The second segment explores working with multiple neurotransmitters and microbiota.

I want to make an important caveat as well. While I've written this chapter to share how to work with the biology of your body, I've also share it in such a way that there isn't a step-by-step process. This is because the process is personalized to each person. What works for me may not be what your body and you need. So this is presented with ideas to make you think as you develop this work and your relationship with your body.

Working with Individual Neurotransmitters and Microbiota

You will find that the majority of the initial work you do will be with individual neurotransmitters and microbiota. This is because when you work with them individually, a simple tweak or adjustment may be all you need to accomplish what you desire.

You have the method for connecting with and establishing a relationship with the individual neurotransmitters and microbiota. Once you have made the connection and established the relationship, the way this process works becomes very simple. You simply use the anthropomorphic or non-anthropomorphic meditation to connect with the relevant spirit and then you start working on making the changes you need to make. I prefer the non-anthropomorphic approach because it really taps into the actual sensation of the spirit you're working with and allows you to communicate with it on its level, which is important because it can show you what it does for your body.

Also, there is an interesting aspect to this work which must be noted. As you work with the neurotransmitter and microbiota spirits more and more you'll find that you access them without thinking about it. This is because as you develop the communication, especially on their terms, they'll end up responding to you and adjusting accordingly to circumstances. This isn't to say that you won't still need to work with them consciously, but rather that the communication will sync over time and you'll find that sometimes they will adjust without you having to consciously decide it. This is useful because then your body adapts to situations more quickly.

So with all that said let's get to some examples so that you can start developing your own individual workings.

Stomach Bacteria and Digestion

As you know, your Stomach Bacteria helps you digest food. In fact without them you couldn't really digest food. Wouldn't it be nice to have an iron stomach, where you could digest most anything and process the food efficiently? Well, with the Stomach Bacteria you can. Because they help you digest food and start the waste removal process, it's worth it to cultivate a relationship with them where you help them understand what you need while also setting the balance with them so you don't get obese or sick. Too many can be hazardous, but enough can help you digest food and might be able to help in cases.

When I first started working with my Stomach Bacteria I connected through the sensation of hunger and feeding. I felt how they became more active when it was time to eat while feeling how they processed and digested food, sharing the nutrients with the body while also sustaining themselves. As a result of learning this information I worked some changes in my physiology so that I could digest food better. I also reduced the number of bacteria, which helped with some weight issues I was having for a time.

So, if you were to apply this to yourself you would connect with the bacteria and from it you would learn what it does and what it could do. Then you would work with it to make adjustments. You'll find as you do this work that the spirits you work with are amendable to needed changes because it ultimately benefits them as much as you. For instance, while my work with bacteria reduced the population this is healthier for the long- term benefits of my body and for the bacteria.

Getting Better Sleep

Whether you suffer from insomnia or just need to go to sleep at a different time of day, knowing how to work your neurochemistry can save you from sleepless nights. When I had to change my lifestyle from being a night owl to doing a first shift job, I did it by working with Melatonin, which is the neurotransmitter responsible for helping you go to sleep.

I use the sensation of feeling tired and a sense of heavy drowsiness to connection with Melatonin. The way Melatonin works is gradual, yet insistent, a siren song that lures you to sleep. If you simply allow yourself to feel that siren song it will ease away the tension and restlessness and induce a state of deep, restorative sleep. When I started working with Melatonin intentionally it supported me in getting deeper sleep by helping me relax into sleep instead of trying to force myself to sleep.

If you apply this to yourself, you want to connect with Melatonin and allow it lead you into sleep. It will do so gently, yet insistently. Simply focus on the sensation of drowsiness and tiredness and you will find yourself falling deep asleep.

Pain Relief

The experience of pain is important in terms of identifying a symptom of something wrong. Nonetheless, it can also be useful to sometimes find a way to mitigate that pain or stop it altogether. Now of course we do have things such aspirin for that purpose with headaches, but sometimes we don't have aspirin or the pain we're dealing with is different than what a given medicine may treat. One of the neurotransmitters I work with for pain relief is Neurokinin A because it helps with inflammation and pain.

If I've had a hard workout or gotten hurt I employ the feeling of Neurokinin A, which is a sense of contraction and smoothing out to where I feel the pain and inflammation. It reduces the pain and inflammation and sometimes gets rid of it altogether. It's particularly helpful for getting pain under control after getting injured.

If you apply Neurokinin A to yourself you don't want to over use it because elevated levels can play a role in fibromyalgia and epilepsy. It's an example of where too much of a good thing can be unhealthy for you. Nonetheless, working with neurokinin when you are in a lot of pain can help you reduce the pain and heal more quickly from inflammation. Focus on that feeling of contraction and smoothing out, or on the Neurokinin A coming in and easing out the tension of the pain and inflammation.

Staying Healthy

One of the ways I stay healthy is employing Mucus as an early warning system. When the Mucus starts flowing more it means my body is getting sick and needs to fight something off. The sensation of Mucus is flow and what I do is encourage it to flow more so that it can help in quickly getting of anything in the respiration system that doesn't belong. Of course, I also focus on getting the Mucus out of my body by hacking and blowing it out. But the more it flows, the more quickly the illness is processed and released because it has no place to be.

If you apply this to yourself it's important to remember to not get disgusted with Mucus. It's simply one of the ways your body is looking out for you. As a result, the focus of Mucus needs to be on increasing the flow and using it as part of your natural defense against illness. The best way to do this is to form a relationship with Mucus where you allow it to warn you through its sensation of flow, and you increase the flow until the illness is done. Trust your body to take care of you and use what it offers to help you expedite the fight against illness.

Altered States of Consciousness

One of the benefits of working with neurotransmitters consciously is that they can help you achieve altered states of consciousness more easily. If you've struggled with achieving a particular state of consciousness, picking the right neurotransmitter and working with it can help you find that desired state and achieve it. I do recommend doing this work purposely and not just for the fun of it, because if you overuse the neurotransmitters you can develop a tolerance to them which makes it harder to achieve those altered states of consciousness.

I also recommend working with the neurotransmitters individually and not mixing them together, because in some cases you're dealing with wildly different stats of consciousness. For example Dopamine and Endorphins might pair well together, but neither would go well with DMT, because the state of consciousness DMT produces is much different from the other two. Let's look at all three individually.

When working with Dopamine, I feel a sense of tingling pleasure that spreads through the body. It creates a sense of deep relaxation and cuts through tension and stress. It can help a person reach a deep state of meditative consciousness.

When working with Endorphins, I feel a sense of clarity and focus, as well as relaxation. Endorphins kick in when I exercise and provide a way to burn off the stress of the day. In cases of ecstatic ritual, they also help me achieve a deeper state of focused awareness for working with the spirits.

When working with DMT, I feel a shift in space and time. My awareness of each changes and I things in the world I normally filter out. DMT strips off the filters and shows me probabilities and other dimensions. The feeling I get is one of crystalline angles coming together and producing an entirely different world perspective.

If you apply this to yourself, take your time working with each neurotransmitter. Learn how they affect your body and mind. Then apply those states of consciousness to your meditation or magical work. How does each change your awareness of the world? How does it shape the magical work you're doing? How can you work with them to go deeper in your spiritual work?

Increasing Your Cognitive Abilities

One of the benefits of working with neurotransmitters is that you can get their help with boosting your cognition and learning. For example, you can work with Glutamate, which is the most abundant neurotransmitter in the brain. It strengthens the connections between neurons and helps improve your memory and ability to learn. When I work with Glutamate I feel a sensation of connection and bonding occurring. When I apply that to learning or problem solving I find it helps me with the problem solving and learning. I start to see connections and explore angles and I stay open and curious.

If you apply this to yourself you want to work with that sensation of learning and connection because that will connect you with Glutamate. You'll feel your neurons firing more and feel your brain become more active. As a result, you'll find that it becomes easier to learn something new and you'll make connections other people miss. You'll feel sharper and more focused. This is useful for any situation where you need to problem solve or learn something. I've found that it's helped me retain more information than I might otherwise.

Increasing Your Strength When You Need It

At one time I worked at a job where I lifted 50 to 100 pound packages for four hours straight and loaded or unloaded them into trucks. It was hard work and by the end of the shift I was tired. However, there was one thing I did at the beginning of the shift which helped me a lot. I would call up Norepinephrine and infuse my muscles with it to help me do the work and keep me from getting too sore. And it worked really well, because I was able to handle lifting those boxes without getting very sore. Norepinephrine kept me awake and pumped the entire time I lifted those books. The downside was that I was really tired after that 4 hour workout.

You can use Norepinephrine to help you with physical tasks or to keep you amped up and awake. When I work with adrenalin in that way, it feels like a burning sensation that goes through my entire body. I feel more awake and focused. You may have, yourself, experienced Norepinephrine in a moment of crisis when you really needed to be focused and aware, such as handling a car crash or being in a fight or trying to save something. The main difference is that your experience was unconscious, a reaction to a situation, whereas as I'm sharing that you can purposely call up Norepinephrine and work with it in a variety of situations.

If you apply Norepinephrine to yourself, you want to apply that awareness, focus and the feeling of it in your body to yourself. In my case I let my body become infused with Norepinephrine and it feels like my muscles and senses are supercharged. I do want to share a word of caution though. Norepinephrine burns through your body's resources and overusing it can leave you feeling exhausted and cranky. So use it when you need to, but don't overdo it either.

Working with Multiple Neurotransmitters and Microbiota

As you can see, working with singular neurotransmitters and microbiota can be quite useful. However, there is limitation in the sense that you're only working with one. Sometimes you need to work with multiple neurotransmitters and microbiota because the issue you're dealing with is complex. It's important to remember that your body is a complex system and that any such work should be done carefully. Your body is the way it is for a reason, but nonetheless it also has great adaptive capacity and we can work with that system and enhance and improve on it.

As with working with singular neurotransmitters and microbiota you are again relying on that experiential awareness to connect with the neurotransmitter and microbiota, but you need to be able to work with multiple experiences. This isn't as hard as it may sound provided you have already done the necessary work to connect with the neurotransmitter and microbiota. If you've also done further work along the lines of what I've shared above, that work will also be helpful and can be something you build on, in what I share below.

You'll notice that in fact we are building on what was shared above and that's because when we're dealing with the systems in our bodies what we discover is that while a singular change may seem to be all you need, sometimes you can also go much further and may need to in order to generate the desired changes you're looking for.

Digestion and Waste Processing

Digestion and waste processing can involve a number of microbiota and neurotransmitters. While I focused on the Stomach Bacteria as an example of singular work you could do, I find that with digestive and waste work it can be very useful to work with the entire ensemble. I link digestion and waste together because the act of digestion necessarily produces waste and I think if you want to improve your digestion, you may as well improve how your body processes waste.

The microbiota we work with are the Archaea, Protozoa, Stomach Bacteria, and Stomach Fungus. The neurotransmitters we work with are Alanine, Aldosterone, Biotin, Bombesin, Cholecystokinin, Dynorphin, Gastrin, Ghrelin, Glutamine, Hypocretin, Leptin, Motilin and Vasopressin. Finally, Mucus is also worked with. As you can see there's a lot being worked with, so let's explore how we can work with all these moving parts.

The first thing we need to realize is that we don't have to work with all of these microbiota and neurotransmitters at the same time. You may find that you don't work with some of them. Also, in some cases the only work that needs to be done is to simply check in and let the neurotransmitter or microbiota do what it does. You'll know because these spirits do make it clear whether they need to be worked with or not, and also because you tune into your body further and further you'll get an intuitive sense of what needs to be adjusted vs what needs to be left alone.

First and foremost, you'll work with Mucus because it plays an integral role in your ability to process of digestion and waste. It basically provides the lubrication to make it all happen. Your work with Mucus will focus on generating enough to make the digestion and passing of waste as easy as possible.

In the intestines you'll find that the microbiota take on a symbiotic role with each other, balancing each other. When you work with them, you'll want to listen to each and then make sure that the Archaea and Protozoa, Stomach Bacteria and Stomach Fungus cooperate to keep each other in balance. When one becomes too much, the others will act to reduce the one so that the digestion is smooth and you don't have too much making you unhealthy. This is the best way to work with the microbiota, so that they balance each other and work together. Use the sensation of them at work to help you connect and then let them guide you. They will know how much they need to be and when they become too much and need to be regulated.

With the act of digestion you'll work Motilin to help the movement of digestion. Motilin causes the contractions that move your food through the intestines to the kidneys. You can use Motilin to help you with the microbiota, since Motilin is moving the food through where the microbiota are, and it can help you control how fast your food is moved through the digestive track. At the same time, if you want to control your appetite (which is another signal to your microbiota) it can be useful to work with Bombesin, Ghrelin, Hypocretin, and Leptin which help regulate your appetite. They tell your digestion when you're full or when you need to put food in your body. You can ask them to help you control your appetite and signal to you when you've had enough. You'll find that when you work with them it's helpful to also work with Gastrin, because they play a role in stimulating Gastrin when you get hungry. Gastrin is what primes the digestive and waste treatment parts of your body. Part of working with Gastrin is simply letting it do what it does, but you'll find that it works with Motilin because of how Motilin prompts the movement of digestion. Gastrin signals hunger and Motilin makes the digestion happen. And you begin to perhaps see how all of this is an inter-related system that you're working with, and how careful you may need to be with that system.

Let's turn to the waste process which naturally occurs as a result of digestion. I recommend working with Aldosterone because it protects the organs that handle waste while also regulating waste. Glutamine is also helpful for regulating the waste processing. Vasopressin can help with kidney functions and processing urine, while Alanine helps the liver filter waste. You'll find that when you work with them together they'll have suggestions for how you can process your waste more efficiently. Working with them will allow you to eat better and make sure you protect your body from the resultant waste.

When you work with each of them you'll ask them to help you process waste, but also to let you know if you need to make changes to your diet. Your waste can tell you a lot about your diet and what needs to change.

Pain Relief

Pain relief isn't just limited to one neurotransmitter. You can work with multiple ones to help you deal with pain and start the healing processes for your body. The one important thing to remember about pain is that pain is a symptom and so we should pay attention to what it is telling us, but at the same time mitigating pain can make your life much easier.

The neurotransmitters and amino acids we work with are Anandamide, Cortisol, Endorphins, Neurokinin A, and Substance P.

When you are feeling sensations of pain you can work Anandamide and Endorphins to moderate the pain and even induce pleasure sensations to counter the feeling. They are helpful for long term pain management. Cortisol is useful in the short term, especially if the pain comes on suddenly, because it can help counter inflammation, but long-term use isn't recommended because it can increase feelings of anxiety and depression. Likewise, you can use Neurokinin A to help manage inflammation, but as with Cortisol, too much of it can be more harmful than helpful. Keep both Neurokinin A and Cortisol for the immediate need to reduce inflammation. Substance P is your messenger for pain. It'll help you recognize when you are feeling sick and it will help you get things out of your body that shouldn't be there. It also will help you recognize inflammation, and you can use it to tell you when the inflammation has decreased and when to stop working with Neurokinin A and Cortisol as a result.

It is important to be careful with pain relief. While it can be good to not be in pain, sometimes you need the pain to discover what's really wrong. I recommend using pain relief when you've gotten hurt in an accident, but if you're dealing with long term pain, it's better to discover what that pain is really trying to tell you.

Enhancing Your Cognitive Functions

While working with one neurotransmitter can be useful for enhancing the cognitive functions of your brain, there are multiple neurotransmitters you can work with, and all of them can be useful for greatly improving your mental well-being, flexibility and acuity.

The neurotransmitters we work with are Asparagine, Aspartate, Dynorphin, GABA, Glutamate, Glycine, Serotonin, and Tyrosine.

I've worked with all these neurotransmitters to enhance my cognitive abilities and awareness. When I work with Asparagine it's like feeling a crystalline awareness in my mind that regularly sharpens my focus and keeps me mentally honed. Aspartate, Glutamate and Serotonin help with memory retention and can be useful in cases when you are trying to recall an important detail. I've also found them helpful for remembering where I left my keys. They also help with learning new skills. I activate them when I'm learning new tech or a new set of skills or trying to understand something I'm reading. Glycine balances Glutamate so there isn't too much of it in the brain. I use Dynorphin to keep track of the electrical patterns of neurotransmitter firing. GABA can be paired with Dynorphin to make sure the electrical firing of the brain isn't happening too frequently, but instead is happening at the right pace to keep your mind sharp and focused. I use Tyrosine to help handle multi-tasking in situations where more than one task needs to be accomplished at a given time.

As you'll probably notice, this isn't just a matter of going all out with these neurotransmitters. There's still a balancing act that needs to happen and this is because without the requisite balance you can do more harm than good. People often make the mistake of thinking that the removal of safeguards will actually improve their lives, but in such cases where you're tinkering with your neurochemistry, those safeguards are there for a reason and you want to use them to help you enhance your learning and cognition while also enabling you to still learn and think.

Staying Healthy and Fit

Staying healthy and fit can take a lot of work on your part. But working with neurotransmitters and amino acids can make that task easier and enhance the overall enjoyment of your life. When I think about health and fitness I don't just think of exercising, but also meditation, so for this section we'll explore how neurotransmitters and amino acids can be applied to either activity.

For physical fitness, the neurotransmitters and amino acids we work with are Acetylcholine, Alanine, Aldosterone, Dopamine, Endorphins, Epinephrine, GABA, Leucine, and Phenethylamine.

For meditation, the neurotransmitters and amino acids we work with are Anandamide, Betalipotropin, Dopamine, and Endorphins.

With physical fitness we want to work with neurotransmitters and amino acids that help with the movement of the muscles and the processing of toxins released by the muscles. Acetylcholine is used to help activate the movement of muscles in exercising. I pair it with Epinephrine (adrenalin) to help warm up the muscles quickly so they don't get strained in the wrong way by the exercise. I also bring GABA into the mix because of how GABA helps the muscles tone. In fact, GABA always indicates to me when it's time to increase the weights I lift or swim longer because it knows what my muscles can take. Alanine, with Aldosterone, purifies the toxins from the muscles, so you want to work with them during and after exercising so that they can get rid of the toxins that the muscles have released. I recommend working with Dopamine, Endorphins and Phenethylamine to help you generate pleasure that can be used as a motivation to keep exercising. I've found that when I've enhanced the release of these neurotransmitters during any physical activity it sharpens my mind and makes me more likely to continue exercising. After I've exercised, I deploy Leucine to help the muscles heal and recover more quickly from exercise. This allows me to build physical strength faster as a result.

Betalipotropin is primarily used to stimulate the creation of other neurotransmitters that can induce altered states of consciousness. When working with Betalipotropin in that way you'll direct it to the pituitary gland so that it can stimulate the productions of the Endorphin neurotransmitters. Endorphins, Dopamine, and Anandamide can be useful for helping you achieve deeper state of meditations because the effect they have is to induce mild states of pleasure. In such a state your mind is more receptive and can achieve deeper states of altered consciousness, which allows you to achieve meditation easier. I actually purposely exercise before meditation because it helps stimulate the neurotransmitters as well, and because when your body has worked out it also makes it easier to quiet the mind and go deep.

Sexual Activity

Whether you want more or less sex, knowing how to increase or decrease your sexual drive can be very helpful. We have a number of neurotransmitters which can help us with either choice and its worth knowing that you can make such a choice for your mental and physical well-being.

The neurotransmitters we work with for increasing or decreasing sexual activity are Dopamine, Endorphins, Estrogen, Gonadotropin, Neurokinin B, Norepinephrine, Oxytocin, Testosterone and Vasopressin.

Most people will think of automatically increasing sexual activity with these neurotransmitters and Amino Acids for more pleasure, but it's also useful to know when to decrease your sexual activity, especially if you're in a situation where you're feeling a lot of frustration and tension. I recommend always keeping in mind that it's not the quantity of sex, but the quality of sex that matters.

Dopamine and Endorphins, as with other activities in the body, induce pleasure and feelings of well-being. They can enhance your general enjoyment of sex. To increase or decrease your sex drive you can work with Estrogen, Gonadotropin, Neurokinin B (which also regulates the release of other sexual neurotransmitters) and Testosterone. To increase or decrease your sex drive you'll simply work with them to adjust the levels of the neurotransmitters that are present in your body. You'll want to make sure you understand how they interact with each other before doing this work. In the case of Estrogen and Testosterone it's important to remember that all people, regardless of sex, have these neurotransmitters and they can also be worked with to help you align to your gender identity. To help you become aroused you can work with Estrogen, Norepinephrine, Testosterone and Vasopressin. Again, when you work with these neurotransmitters together you'll want to see how they connect together and work off of each other to help you increase or decrease your arousal. To help you with emotional bonding and deeper intimate connection during and after sex I recommend working with Oxytocin. The act of cuddling will automatically increase its presence in your body, but you can also work with it on your own to increase the feeling and this can help induce a state of deep contentment.

Handling Stress

Stress is a regular part of life, but knowing how to handle it is key to whether you live a healthy life or an unhealthy life, whether you are happy or miserable. Now part of how you handle stress is simply through your attitude toward life and whether you take a glass half-full or half-empty approach, but part of it is also based on your neurochemistry and how you work with it.

The neurotransmitters we work with for handling stress are Anandamide, Arginine, Corticotrophin, Dopamine, Endorphins, Epinephrine, GABA, Niacin, Norepinephrine, Oxytocin, Proline, and Serotonin.

In stressful situations what you may first need, depending on the situation, is Corticotrophin, Epinephrine and Norepinephrine. They are very useful in survival situations because they allow you to use your reflexes to figure out a possible solution. Use them sparingly and carefully because they really are meant for survival situations. Anandamide, Dopamine, and Endorphins help you handle stress by increasing pleasure and decreasing stress. Oxytocin helps you reduce stress by bringing you feelings of belonging. It can be worked with in conjunction with the previous three neurotransmitters, but it can also be worked with on its own and is particularly helpful for dealing with feelings of anxiety. When dealing with physical aspects of stress such as increased blood pressure and high cholesterol, working with Arginine and Niacin can help you manage these symptoms and get your body back to a better state of health without overtaxing your system. GABA and Serotonin can help you manage feelings of anxiety and depression that may come up as a result of stress, bringing you to a place of calm, focused awareness for dealing with any situation.

Fighting Off Sickness/Staying Healthy

Staying healthy and fighting off sickness is partially a matter of lifestyle choices. Are you getting enough sleep and are you eating right, exercising, and otherwise taking care of your health? Still, while those are factors, your neurotransmitters and microbiota can also be worked with to improve your health. In fact, I've worked with my extensively to help me with my health and it's improved my quality of life while also getting preventing me from getting sick.

The microbiota we work with are Skin Bacteria and Fungus, as well as Mucus.

The neurotransmitters we work with are Aldosterone, Arginine, Biotin, Dopamine, Dynorphin, Enkephalin, Histamine, Histidine, Insulin, Isoleucine, Lysine, Niacin, and Secretin.

You'll want to work with the microbiota carefully. While they can help you fight off infections, they can also become the invader. For example, staph infections occur when your Skin Bacteria infects an open wound. Normally Skin Bacteria protects you, but in the case of a staph infection its purpose is subverted. Likewise Skin Fungus can help protect you, but too much can cause issues like athlete's foot. My suggestion in working with them is to employ them to help you take care of your skin and protect your body from foreign microbiota, but also know when to rein them in. You can work with Lysine to help you with the microbiota sense, as Lysine's focus is on the health of your skin. Lysine can be used to monitor the microbiota and make sure they are performing their functions. Working with Mucus is helpful in cases of proactively getting front of illnesses such as colds. The key is to use

Mucus as an early warning system and get it out of your body so you don't get an upper respiratory infection.

In the body neurotransmitters and amino acids help you fight off sickness and stay healthy by acting as early warning systems and mobilizing your immune system. The neurotransmitters and amino acids you want to work with as early warning systems are Enkephalin and Histamine, while also working with histidine to produce more Histamine. Histamine will trigger allergies, allowing you to recognize what you are allergic to, while Enkephalin helps you recognize when something makes you nauseous and can prompt you to throw up. While this might seem like a negative, we need to remember that the body has these systems in place to protect itself and, as such, working with them can help you get sickness out of your body sooner.

To mobilize and improve your immune system you want to work with Aldosterone, Arginine, Biotin, Dopamine, Dynorphin, Insulin, Isoleucine, Niacin, and Secretin. Each of these neurotransmitters and amino acids can help you regulate your immune system while also taking care of the organs of your body and regulating blood pressure. These various tasks will help you protect the health of your body and may help you live longer. When you work with these spirits you may find that they point you toward lifestyle changes. You'll also find that they all work together. They are part of an intricate system of health in your body that works to take care of your body and regulate your body. You don't necessarily want to make radical changes. You want to work with them and rely on them to help you know your body better. Trust their suggestions and implement them and you'll see an improvement. Your body, after all, knows best when it comes to its own health.

Conclusion

What I've shared here is just the tip of the iceberg of how you can work with the spirits of your body to take care of your health and improve your well-being. I recommend that you consider your own circumstances and find out which of the spirits applies to those circumstances and then start getting to know them and work with them. For example, if you have cancer, then working with some of these spirits may help you mitigate the effects of the cancer or even heal it. Regardless of what your situation is, you'll only know how these spirits can help you if you do the work.

You'll also notice in the sections above that while I have provided you some ideas on how to work with these spirits of the body, I haven't told you what to specifically do, and there are a couple good reasons for that. The first reason is because your body may be different from mine and, as a result, what you need may be different. You might need to stimulate hunger more, for example, whereas I need to control my appetite. The second reason is that it's important for you to go into this work without preconceived notions of what to expect. You're going to connect with these spirits and they will help you understand what needs to be changed. It's not a matter of controlling them, so much as working with them and, as such, I've purposely left this work a bit vague so that it's not prescriptive. So you actually do the requisite work of creating the relationships with care and consideration given to what is healthy for your body and you.

One other thing I want to mention is that as you work with these spirits further you'll find that the work starts happening intuitively. Initially you'll need to consciously connect with them and then, as you strengthen that connection, the work will happen on a deeper level. This makes sense because you are entering into a deeper symbiotic relationship with your body. The life within your body will respond to your efforts and as your relationship grows stronger, the spirits will work on that deeper level. You'll find yourself prompted to make changes to your lifestyle, and if you trust your body and the spirits within, those changes will greatly enhance your life. If you don't develop that relationship then you'll be much like any other person who hasn't taken the time to really know their body. When you are out of touch and unaware, then surprises happen and usually they aren't good for you.

Chapter 7 Executive Dysfunctions and the Inner Alchemy of Life

One of the benefits of working with the neurotransmitters is that you can not only apply neurotransmitters to your body, but also to the health of your mind. We live in a world that is increasingly stressful and causes people to feel heightened anxiety and depression. The trauma that we live can cause what is known as executive dysfunction. Executive dysfunction is a general term that describes cognitive, emotional, and behavioral issues that people experience, sometimes linked to brain injury, but sometimes also linked to environmental aspects that a person deals with in life. In this chapter I will show you how working with neurotransmitters can be applied to different types of executive dysfunction, and how they can potentially mitigate or even heal the effects of these types of executive dysfunctional. Please keep in mind that if you are taking medicine to treat a mental issue, you should continue to do so until you've been instructed otherwise by your doctor.

Anxiety Disorder

There are a variety of anxiety disorders including General Anxiety Disorder, Social Anxiety Disorder, Separation Anxiety Disorder, Phobias, and Panic Disorder. All of these can be characterized as anxiety disorders because a person feels anxiety and stress, though how that anxiety and stress is expressed can differ depending on the condition. People who have Generalized Anxiety Disorder have consistent feelings of anxiety, worry and fear that isn't focused on specific subject, but instead is generalized. Along with these feelings they may be restless and have trouble sleeping. In contrast, people who have Social Anxiety Disorder feel significant anxiety in social situations and may have physical symptoms that include itching, blushing, and sweating. People with Separation Anxiety Disorder feel extreme anxiety when they leave their home or are away from their loved ones, while people with Phobias feel intense fear and anxiety about something in particular such as a fear of being outside or a fear of a specific type of animal. People who have Panic Disorders experience panic attacks because of environmental stress, which causes them to feel fear and anxiety as well as physical symptoms including sweating, shaking, shortness of breath and a feeling that something awful is going to happen. While the symptoms of these disorders may vary, what all of them have in common is that a feeling of extreme anxiety and fear effects the person.

If you experience one of these disorders in your life I do recommend continuing to work with your doctor on whatever prescribed course of action has been developed. Let's look at how we can work with our neurotransmitters to either mitigate or possibly cure these conditions.

You'll want to work on increasing the neurotransmitter GABA. People who suffer from any of these disorders typically have lower levels of GABA in their brains, so the increase of GABA can help immensely because it inhibits the overall activity of the neurons. When you work with GABA, get its guidance for where it needs to go in the brain. You'll likely find that a lot of it will need to go to the amygdala, which controls the stress and fear responses we have. You may also find sending GABA to the hypothalamus, cerebellum and brain stem is helpful because these areas are directly affected by the amygdala.

While you increase GABA you may also want to reduce the levels of anxiety neurotransmitters Corticotrophin and Cortisol. You'll also want to work with Serotonin and Norepinephrine, specifically on adjusting the uptake cycle that they have in the brain. In this case you'll ask them to slow that uptake cycle down so that they stay in the brain longer, stabilizing emotional moods. You might also work with Endorphins, Dopamine and Oxytocin which can provide you experience of pleasure and closeness that counteract feelings of anxiety and worry. Oxytocin, in particular, can help combat feelings of stress and anxiety because of the sensation of belonging and community it induces.

What's most important is that you realize that anxiety doesn't have to define your life. Making the changes I've shared above can help out immensely. In situations where I've felt lots of anxiety and fear I've done the changes I mentioned above and found that the anxiety and fear became much more manageable, and that I could, as a result, start making changes in my life to address the cause of those feelings.

Depression

Depression generally comes in two flavors. You have clinical depression, where a person is always feeling depressed and you have bipolar depression, where a person alternately feels depression or a sense of manic happiness. In either case, it can cause a person a lot of misery and unhappiness. As I've shared before, I've had my own experiences with depression and when I changed my neurochemistry with the neurotransmitters that stopped. Depending on what kind of depression you have, you'll find that you'll take different approaches. As I've stated about, if you are on medicine or seeing a therapist continue doing so.

With clinical depression, the approach you'll want to take will involve working with Serotonin, specifically to slow down the uptake cycle, which will keep Serotonin in your brain longer. You might also work with Norepinephrine in a similar manner. I'd also recommend working with Endorphins and Dopamine to stimulate pleasure and help you find enjoyment in different activities. You might also work with Melatonin, to help you sleep, which can help counteract depression, if you're not getting enough sleep.

With bipolar disorder, you have to take a different approach depending on whether you're depressed or manic. When you're depressed you want to work with Serotonin and Norepinephrine to slow down the uptake cycle, which will help balance your moods. In the manic phase you want to reduce the amount of Dopamine and Glutamate, which will help moderate the manic phase. You may also want to increase the uptake cycle for Tyrosine, which will also help moderate the manic phase.

In the case of both of these disorders, it really comes down to understanding the right mix of neurotransmitters can have a favorable effect on your neurochemistry, which will help moderate your depression or possibly cure it. However, this doesn't mean you'll never experience depression. Even though I've used neurotransmitters to help me with the bipolar depression I experienced, I still get depressed sometimes. However, when I get depressed it's not because of neurochemistry being off, but rather is because it's a natural response to a situation, such as feeling sad or unhappy about bad news.

Attention Deficit Hyperactivity Disorder

Attention Deficit Hyperactivity Disorder (ADHD) is characterized by hyperactivity, where a person feels the need to move or shows excessive fidgeting, and an inability to pay attention for any length of time to activities that don't interest a person, and impulsive behavior where the person engages in actions without recognizing the ramifications of those actions. It's typically treated as a disorder because the person isn't paying attention in a way that conforms to societal expectations. A person with ADHD may be considered mentally and/ or physically restless, unable to pay attention, unable to focus on details and other symptoms that generally demonstrate an inability to focus. There is also internalized ADHD, where the person doesn't display hyperactivity, but does have an inability to pay attention or finish tasks, and may seem to be withdrawn.

Usually ADHD is treated through drugs such as Ritalin, which are used to force the person to focus. However one does have to question if ADHD is really a disorder since kids, as an example, are typically hyperactive, which is appropriate for their age, and because we live in an oversaturated environment with lots of distraction and an encouragement to multi-task which actually takes away from being able to focus and attend to details.

If a person does want to find a way to use neurotransmitters to help them with their ADHD the following practice may yield some useful results (and is worth exploring). With ADHD, we would look at changing the uptake cycles (how quickly or slowly a neurotransmitter is processed) and levels of Dopamine, Norepinephrine, Serotonin, Achetylcholine, and Glutamate, because these neurotransmitters can affect parts of the brain that are impacted by ADHD. Additionally, we would work with the systems of the brain that are affected by ADHD, such as the accumbens, amygdala, cuadate, hippocampus, and putamen in order to improve the efficacy of those systems and even help with creating new neural pathways that strengthen those parts of the brain. You'll work with the neurotransmitters to effect those parts of your brain and create the necessary activity that adjust the electrochemistry.

So how does all of this work? First, you need to connect with the neurotransmitters and create relationships with them. Then, you would work directly with them to change the uptake cycle, as well as any other aspects of your neurochemistry they suggested you would want to change. This could be done through meditation, using breath work to connect with the body. If that didn't work, I'd alternately suggest pathworking and/or using an external system such as tarot to simulate the environment and create a causal link that could be used to connect with the neurotransmitters.

Once that work was done, you'd focus next on the brain and the specific subsystems affected by ADHD. Your goal would be to stimulate additional neural pathways and to grow each of those systems so that they could help with the regulation of attention. You'd also connect with the body and see if there was any tension that need to be expressed or movement that needed to be realized or any food desired, because sometimes those things can also prove helpful.

I am not diagnosed with ADHD, so I can't say for sure that my suggested methodology would work. I do, at times, have issues with my attention span and when I recognize my attention is wandering, I stop trying to write and meditate for a bit, focusing on my brain and stimulating the parts of the brain that help with focus. That does seem to help me get the focused attention I need.

But again, I've never been diagnosed with ADHD so I can't say for sure if it would or wouldn't work. I would point out there is no harm in trying and seeing what happens. If you're taking medicine to manage your ADHD I don't recommend going off of it, but if you try to do some workings along the lines I've proposed, keep track of what you're doing and see if it enhances the effect of the medicine or if you notice that you feel sharper and more focused with the combination of medicine and the proposed magical work here.

Obsessive-Compulsive Disorder

Obsessive-Compulsive Disorder (OCD) is a disorder where a person has uncontrollable, reoccurring thoughts (obsessions) and behaviors (compulsions). A couple of examples are when a person feels a need to obsessively clean themselves or make sure everything is setup a certain way or do activities in a specific routine obsessively and can't stop or control this behavior very easily. As mentioned above, if you are being treated for OCD, please keep using your treatment in tandem with anything you choose to do here.

In the brain, when someone is experiencing OCD there is abnormal activity in the orbitofrontal cortex, which is responsible for decision making. Additionally the prefrontal and premotor cortexes also seem to be affected.

The neurotransmitters you'll want to work with are Serotonin, Dopamine and Glutamate. However you'll want to be careful how you work with them, because there's not an easy or pat answer for how they'll effect you. For instance, in some cases more Serotonin is helpful, and in other cases less Serotonin seems to be helpful. Slowing the uptake cycle of Dopamine does seem to help manage OCD symptoms. In the case of Glutamate, as with Serotonin, you'll need to carefully test and determine whether you need to slow the uptake cycle or increase it. I recommend with all of these neurotransmitters taking a cautious approach and finding out from them what is needed in order to help you manage the OCD.

Schizophrenia

Schizophenia is a disorder where a person can experience visual and auditory hallucinations and delusions of paranoia and fear. Additionally, a person who has Schizophrenia can have difficulty taking care of themselves both in terms of hygiene and in the ability to make decisions. A person with schizophrenia may also feel emotions less and have difficulty speaking or engaging in activities.

It's been found that people who have schizophrenia have high levels of Dopamine in their brain and low levels of Glutamate. Additionally, the brain in a schizophrenic person gradually grows smaller.

In this case, a person with schizophrenia would want to reduce the levels of Dopamine in the brain by increasing the uptake cycle for Dopamine while also working on increase the level of Glutamate so the two balance each other out. You would also want to work with GABA in a similar capacity in order to control the firing other neurons. Doing this should help mitigate the hallucinations the person experiences and may counteract the overall negative effects. Please continue any treatment plan you're on.

Post-Traumatic Stress Disorder

Post-Traumatic Stress Disorder (PTSD) occurs when a person has experienced a traumatic event(s) in their life. While PTSD is typically associated with warfare, a person who's has abusive or sexual assault experiences, or an event such as a car accident or any other type of threat on one's life can have PTSD. When you have PTSD you can be triggered by noises or activities that cause you to experience flashbacks to the original traumatic event. Not everyone who experiences a traumatic event will have PTSD. Usually it occurs in interactional situations, where violence has been committed by one person to another (or more than one).

PTSD affects the body by causing an abnormal amount of adrenalin to flow through the body, causing the person to experience intense moments of the fight or flight response, where the response is either to fight or flee the stressful situation a person is in. People with PTSD have low levels of Cortisol and high levels Norepinephrine in the body. PTSD also effects the limbic and amygdala systems of the brain which regulate emotions. A person with PTSD will also have low levels of Serotonin and Dopamine in the brain.

In the case of PTSD what you'll want to do is reduce the levels of Norepinephrine in the body while increasing the levels of Cortisol. Cortisol helps with stress response and handling how you respond to stress while Norepinephrine (adrenalin) will increase the flight or fight response which can induce the symptoms of PTSD. In the brain you'll want to increase the uptake cycle for Serotonin and Dopamine, particularly in the limbic and amygdala systems of the brain. By doing that you'll prolong the time the neurotransmitters in your brain, which reduce the anxiety and stress that you're experiencing.

I've had my own experiences of PTSD due to traumatic events in my life and I found that when I worked with the neurotransmitters, the intense feelings of anxiety and stress decreased and the flashbacks to the moments of trauma were decreased. It also made it easier for me to work through those experiences and start finding some peace with what happened.

If you're already on existing treatment plan, please continue that plan while working with your neurotransmitters.

Conclusion

I want to say in closing that I've not been diagnosed with all of these conditions. I was diagnosed with Bipolar 2 depression and I've had experience with anxiety, as well as some PTSD from traumatic childhood and early adulthood events. In those cases I've shared my own treatment as it were, which has helped me either heal or mitigate the symptoms. In other cases, such as with OCD and ADHD, I've shared some possible ideas about what you could do, but don't take my word for it. If you live with either of those or something else, you know it better than I do, so take what I've shared with a grain of salt. The best thing you can do is connect with the neurotransmitters and work with them to determine what to adjust or change. And, as I've said above, if you are already pursuing a treatment plan, stick with it and measure what you're doing against it so you can verify if what you're doing is generating results.

It's my hope that this chapter shows how a person can affect their neurochemistry by working with the neurotransmitters, and at the same time be reminded that we don't have to let what we're diagnosed with define our lives. Instead we can choose to work with our bodies and discover solutions that empower all of us.

Conclusion

This is a book which has been on my mind, literally and figuratively, for a while. I've been meaning to write it for years, but a lot of stuff got in the way until that stuff got cleared out and this book grabbed by the scruff of my neck and said, "Write me already damnit!" And now it's written. When I wrote *Inner Alchemy* and shared my work the neurotransmitters, it was really only the beginning of this work. What I've shared here is a continuance and deepening of that work.

I'm not alone in being fascinating with working with the body. If you look at Taoist practices, for example, you'll find a rich body of lore and practices that explores how to cultivate the internal energy of the body while improving the health of the body. And there are other practices that take similar approaches. However, what I think makes my work unique is that what I've shared here is how to actually work with aspects of the body we take for granted. And these aspects, the neurotransmitters and microbiota of life within us, are typically ignored in spiritual practices because they aren't easy to see or recognize, yet they are in the background of our lives keeping us alive.

Everyday our body runs itself for all intents and purposes. The bacteria in our body helps us digest food and process waste, while the neurotransmitters regulate our body functions and emotions. Yet we take all of this for granted. It's just part of being human, and unless you get a disease or get sick, you don't put much thought toward the miracle of life that makes your life possible.

My hope is that with this book you'll start thinking differently about your body and start trying to communicate with it on a deeper level by working with the bacteria and neurotransmitters, the fungus and amino acids, and, as a result, perhaps achieve a deeper level of connection with the Earth as well. You see, one reason I've done this work is because I found that when I started looking at my relationship with my body and stopped taking the life within it for granted, that's when I started changing my relationship with the environment around me. And it makes sense. How can you effectively take care of the world around you if you don't take care of the world within you?

I would urge you to think of this book as a beginning, because that's what it is. It's the beginning of a new relationship you'll have with your body and life, if you choose to do the work.

I am already writing the next book *The Inner Alchemy of Breath and Sound*, which will explore the relationship of breath and sound with the body, but also explore the experiential relationship the body has with the environment. The relationship you cultivate with your body happens on multiple levels, and the key to living a healthy life is exploring as many of those levels as possible and gaining a deeper understanding of our body in the process. Hopefully this book will you help with that process.

Taylor Ellwood
Portland, Oregon
November, 2018

Want more Inner Alchemy?

You can order your digital copies from me directly. Order your copies at https://www.magicalexperiments.com/inner-alchemy-series

Appendix 1: DNA and RNA Magical Workings

I began working with the elements of DNA around the time I did my first working with Serotonin. I was fascinated with working with the body and it made sense to me that I should work with DNA and RNA because of the role both play in the body. In this appendix I'll share the work I've done with each, as well as the purpose of the work.

My Work with DNA

The work I did focused on establishing a connection with DNA and determining if a correspondence with the classic elemental energy of Air, Fire, Water and Earth could be established. I'll admit that the connection was fairly arbitrary. I associated specific elemental energies with DNA and RNA and for all intents and purposes it seemed to work. The correspondences are as follows Guanine = Earth, Adenine = Air, Cytosine = Fire, Thymine = Water, and Uracil = Spirit. In the workings I did I visualized that I visited each DNA and RNA strand and embedded the hermetic symbol for each element on the appropriate DNA/RNA strand. Eventually, I changed this embedded all of the hermetic symbols on each strand because I realize that an elemental attribution to one strand was a limitation.

The purpose for doing that work was to build off previous work I had done where I'd given blood to the elements in return for deeper access to the elemental energies. My rationale for this work was that by embedding the hermetic symbols of the elemental energies I could strengthen the connection with the elemental energies even further, tying them to my life force and magic, so that I could draw on them more effectively.

I did find that after doing this work it seemed I had a deeper connection to the elemental energies. I found that I could tap into and connect with the elemental currents of energy even easier than

I had before. This helped in particular with weather magic, but also with some healing workings, because of the way the elemental energies can be used to balance the internal energy of the body. I also felt that since DNA contains the biological information for the body there's no reason not to add to that information with spiritual biology so to speak. I've since replicated this process with other types of spiritual energies and have found it to be useful for creating that deeper connection with those energies.

The way it works is that you do need to establish a connection with the DNA and RNA elements while also having a connection with the spiritual energies you want to mesh with the DNA and RNA. I suggest doing a pathworking with the DNA/RNA, where you visualize embedding a symbol which represents the spiritual energy into the DNA and RNA. What this allows you to do is connect those energies with your body, allowing them to become part of the biology of your body on a spiritual level.

That's the work I've done with the DNA. In general, everything else I've done with the body has either been with the cells directly or with the neurotransmitters and bacteria of the body. I think the DNA, by its very nature, is really designed to be a storehouse of information. We can add to that storehouse for our own purposes, but we are still nonetheless the human because that's what the DNA designs us to be.

Appendix 2: The Spirituality of this Work

I've spent the majority of this book describing the theoretical and practical aspects of working with the neurotransmitters and microbiota of your body. What I haven't really discussed are the spiritual dimensions. I'll admit that in general my work tends to be very focused toward the practical end of magic, but there is a spiritual dimension to this work and I want to discuss and describe it here.

The purpose of this book is to help you create and cultivate a healthier relationship with your body and the life within you that makes your life possible. You may have noticed that the focus of this work emphasizes working with the life in your body, as opposed to trying to command it. This is purposeful because I think as human beings we must learn how to develop a more purposeful relationship with our bodies that is respectful of the life within, and that I hope teaches us to also be respectful of our place on this world and in the universe.

In general, I find that people seem to oblivious to the long-term impact of their choices on this world, yet can most people be faulted when they are also oblivious to the long-term impact of their choices on themselves? Perhaps. The sad reality is that many people choose to blind themselves to their choices, both in terms of how they treat their bodies and how they treat the world around them.

The spiritual aspect of this work is driven by the realization that if people want to change their relationship with the Earth or the universe, they must also learn how to change their relationship with the bodies they inhabit.

So what does that mean and how does this work apply?

When you go on this journey with your body and start interacting with the life within, as well as just learning how to connect with your body, you'll find that it causes you to start examining what you put into your body and how you take care of yourself. From that seed of awareness, what also changes is your relationship with the environment around you. For when you recognize how you affect your body with your choices you also begin to discover how you affect the world around you. What happens in the microcosm is also expressed in the macrocosm, and vice versa.

I think if people learn to have healthier relationships with their bodies they might also learn to have healthier relationships with the world around them. Certainly, this has been the case for me as a result of doing this work and related work.

The spirituality of this work is found in the rhythm and communication of your body, in the experience of your body speaking to you through the life within, and through learning to listen and not just command your body. Open yourself to the experiences of your body, and what will change is not just your relationship with it and the life within, but also the world around you. If you've done the work, you already know what I'm sharing here, and if you haven't, then I invite you to do so.

Bibliography

Abram, David. (1997). *The spell of the sensuous: Perception and language in a more-than-human world*. New York: Vintage Books.

Ackerman, Jennifer. (2007). *Sex sleep eat drink dream*. New York: Houghton Mifflin Company.

Blaser, Martin J. (2014). *Missing microbes: How the overuse of antibiotics is fueling our modern plagues*. New York: Henry Holt and Company.

Brennan, Barbara Ann. (1988). *Hands of light: A guide to healing through the human energy field*. New York: Bantam Books.

Brennan, Barbara Ann. (1993). *Light emerging: the journey of personal healing*. New York: Bantam Books.

Frantzis, B. K. (2001). *Relaxing into your being: Breathing, chi, & dissolving the ego*. Berkeley: North Atlantic Books.

Frantzis, B. K. (2001). *The great stillness: Body awareness, moving meditation, & sexual chi gung*. Berkeley: North Atlantic Books.

Frantzis, Bruce. (2009). *Tao of letting go: Meditation for modern living*. Berkeley: North Atlantic Books.

LeDoux, Joseph. (2002). *Synaptic self: How our brains become who we are*. New York: Penguin Books.

Lilly, John C. (2004). *Programming the human biocomputer.* Berkeley: Ronin Publishing, Inc.

Lipton, Bruce. (2005). *The biology of belief: Unleashing the power of consciousness, matter and miracles.* Santa Rosa: Elite Books.

Mace, Stephen. (1984). *Stealing the fire from heaven.* Milford: Self-published.

Maczulak, Anne. (2011). *Allies and enemies: How the world depends on bacteria.* Upper Saddle River: Pearson Education, Inc.

Mindell, Arnold. (1993). *The shaman's body: A new relationship for transforming health, relationships, and the community.* New York: Harper Collins

Mindell, Arnold. (2002). *Working with the dreaming body.* Portland: Lao Tse Press.

Mindell, Arnold. (2002). *Working on yourself alone.* Portland: Lao Tse Press.

Ratey, John J. (2001). *A user's guide to the brain: Perception, attention, and the four theaters of the brain.* New York: Vintage Books.

Shusterman, Richard. (2012). *Thinking through the body: Essays in somaesthetics.* New York: Cambridge University Press.

Tibika, Francoise. (2013). *Molecular consciousness: Why the universe is aware of our presence.* Rochester: Park Street Press.

Want to take your magical practice even further?

If your answer is yes, then you'll want to check out Magical Experiments University[1], where I offer classes on magic. These are video courses where you get a chance to hear and see me instruct you about how magic works and how to get consistent results.

I also have a video course on the practices of this book where I walk you through how to do the meditations.

Sign up for Magical Experiments University[2] today.

---

1. https://magical-experiments.teachable.com/

2.   https://magical-experiments.teachable.com/

You finished Book 2 of the How Inner Alchemy Works Series, but there's more...

The next book in the How Inner Alchemy Works Series is Inner Alchemy of Internal work, where I walk you through how to do internal work through meditation, pathworking and other modalities in order to dissolve your traumas and blockages.

Want to learn more inner alchemy?

Get Inner Alchemy of Internal Work, available through my website[1] and with retailers[2].

---

1.   https://www.magicalexperiments.com/inner-alchemy-series

2.   https://books2read.com/u/47QOxN

About the Author

Taylor Ellwood is the author of numerous books on magic including Pop Culture Magick, Space/Time Magic, and Inner Alchemy. When he isn't working on his latest magical experiment or writing a book he can be found enjoying games, books, and life and the company of his amazing wife. For more information about his latest projects, check out his site http://www.magicalexperiments.com

Want more Inner Alchemy?

An Introduction to Internal Work

I'm not a therapist or a psychologist, so you might be wondering why I'm writing a book on the inner alchemy of internal work. You might also wonder what significance, if any, emotions have in relationship to inner alchemy or magical work. After all, everyone experiences emotions, but not everyone practices magic or necessarily does internal work around their emotions. For that matter, it can be argued that doing any kind of internal work around your emotions isn't really magical work at all. In fact, recently a fellow occult author made the argument that shadow work isn't real magic, it's just a form of psychology. He could have applied that broad brush to all internal work, because in one sense working with our emotions and internal tensions is a form of psychological work, but I'd argue that there's more on going on with internal work than is just found in psychology. When we try to relegate part of our spiritual work to a non-magical discipline, we can make the mistake of pigeonholing that spiritual work and invalidating the ways that work can transform our lives.

What motivates me to write this book and title it *Inner Alchemy of Internal Work* is a recognition that the relationship many of us have with our emotions is dysfunctional at best and yet, I have found that emotions do play a pivotal role in the magical work that people do. Certainly my own emotions have played a role in terms of how they have motivated my choices and empowered my magical workings. Yet writing this book isn't so much about the magic of emotions, as it is about understanding the place of emotions in our magical work, our lives, and in how we can become better people by learning how to develop a proactive approach to working with emotions. That proactive approach is found via internal work, which isn't merely a set of psychological techniques, but also has physiological and energetic components that play pivotal roles in the work we choose to do on ourselves.

Internal work is essential to the path of the magician, but many occultists do not do internal work, preferring instead to either focus on practical magic techniques to get results or working with spirits, and these are relevant spirituals practices to do, but what I find is that internal work balances out the practical magic and work with spirits by grounding us in our identity and allowing us to work through and dissolve the reactions we have, while replacing them with proactive behaviors that allow us to lead better lives. Yet internal work is not easy. In fact, sometimes it is messy because of how we come face to face with the work we necessarily need to do that nonetheless calls on us to work with parts of ourselves that we may find icky, disgusting or loathsome, but which we need to work with.

The most important reason I've chosen to write this book is because of my own relationship with my emotions. I have not always known how to handle my emotions in a way that I would describe as healthy, but as a practitioner of magic, I think it's essential to learn how to handle your emotions, because when you are pulling together a magical working, the emotions you feel play a role in that magical working. To argue otherwise is to delude yourself to an essential reality that all of us have to deal with: When you are alive, you feel something and what you feel can and usually does play a role in the choices and actions you make. Add magic to the mix and it creates that much more complexity in your life.

My *Inner Alchemy* series explores the magic of the body. The emotions we feel are part of the expression and experience of having a body. We might, as spirits, feel emotions as well, but the experience of those emotions are likely different from how we as incarnate beings experience emotions. After all, your emotions, in part, are informed by the physiology of your body. The neurotransmitters and hormones that your body produces play a role in generating the emotional experiences you have, and can even create pre-dispositions toward specific states of consciousness such as depression and mania. At the same time, the emotions we feel can't be solely relegated electro-chemical changes in our neurochemistry. They are responses to the experience of the world we have and they shape our reactions and actions, our thoughts, and our experience of ourselves.

In this book, I'm inviting you to explore your own relationships with your emotions, so that you better understand the role they play in both your magical work and the internal work that can accompany such work. The exploration of that relationship may help you recognize the ways that your emotions show up in your spiritual work and in how you live your life. And while this isn't a book written about the psychology of emotions, it may also help you develop a better relationship with your emotions, which is something most, if not all of us, need. With that said, I will briefly mention again my disclaimer that I am not a therapist, psychologist, or medical professional. If you are on medication, please consult with the appropriate person before engaging in the exercises contained within this book.

I also want to be clear that while a lot of the focus of this book on the emotions, I am also choosing to focus on other aspects of internal work that involve working through thoughts, feelings and tensions, because all of these things contribute to our emotional experiences. Learning to work with them can help us also work through our emotions and allow us to release the tension and stress that otherwise can show up in our lives and sabotage our experiences.

The Difference between Emotions and Feelings

The words emotions and feelings tend to be used interchangeably, but I think it's worthwhile to distinguish between what an emotion seems to be and what a feeling seems to be, because emotions and feelings are not necessarily one and the same thing. You can experience a feeling without necessarily having an emotion accompany it. I can feel a sensation of pain or pleasure in my body and not have an emotional response to that feeling. For example, if you have an itch and you scratch you are responding to the feeling of itchiness, and there may or may not be an emotional response that accompanies your choice to scratch the itch.

In contrast, an emotion is more than just a physical feeling, though it may prompt physical symptoms. When you feel sad, you may or may not cry, but you will still have an experience of sadness that goes beyond just the physical sensations of sadness. That experience of sadness becomes an extension and expression of your identity. This applies to the experiences you have with other emotions as well. The difference between a feeling and an emotion can be simply stated as this: A feeling affects the physical awareness of your body, while your emotions affect your sense of identity and become an expression of that identity, as well as affecting the physical awareness of your body.

In this book, I'm going to primarily use the words emotions because what we're dealing with is this effect on our identities, which is quite significant from a metaphysical perspective, because the identities we maintain bring with them a metaphysical mass that we utilize in our magical workings. In other words, the emotions we experience play a role in the magical work we do, because of how they express our identities into those workings. In my own experiences, I've found that a person's identity plays an integral role in magical work, because of how that identity becomes a vehicle for the changes that a person wants to realize in the world and in themselves (See my book Magical Identity for more information.). The emotions we experience shape our identity in the moment, and can help us have powerful transformative experiences around that sense of identity.

Exercise

What are your definitions of feelings and emotions? Do you think there's a difference between feelings and emotions, and if so how would you delineate that difference? How does that difference effect your understanding of feelings and emotions in relationship to yourself?

Share your answers in the Magical Experiments Facebook group with #IAIW.

The Difference between Emotions and Thoughts

Our emotions and thoughts are not one and the same, though a thought can prompt an emotion and an emotion can prompt a thought. Your thoughts are typically images, words, or a combination of the two and they are how you process and make sense of information, whereas emotions are experiential, felt in your body, but not processed as a thought. You can think about your emotions, which can become a trap in its own right, because thinking about an emotion is not the same as feeling it. Thinking about emotions causes you to analyze them, but analysis isn't necessarily the same as doing internal work around emotions. What can be helpful with thoughts is recognizing how they can take on a life of their own, and learning how to dissolve such thoughts so they don't hijack your life.

Exercise

What are your experiences with thoughts and emotions? How do you differentiate between an emotion and a thought?

Share your answers in the Magical Experiments Facebook group with #IAIW.

The Difference between Emotions and Tensions

In my experience, emotions and tensions tend to go hand in hand, because emotions can become blockages, which are experiences of tension. Nonetheless, not all emotions are automatically tensions. I think of experiences of tension as a blockage that is frozen around an emotional experience or thought that is keeping the person in a place of discomfort and stress. You can have an emotional experience without it becoming tension, provided you are able to relax and release into that emotional experience. You can also dissolve a blockage of tension and allow it to become an emotional experience that you work through and release as you experience it. The majority of blockages are around experiences of trauma, whether its old trauma or new trauma, but blockages don't always have to be related to trauma. What's important to recognize is that you necessarily have to dissolve the blockage in order to release what makes that blockage what it is.

Exercise

What are your experiences of blockages? How do you identify and work through tension and blockages in your body?

Share your answers in the Magical Experiments Facebook group with #IAIW.

Emotions and Identity

I've made the claim above that emotions effect our identities. What does that really mean? What it means is that the experience of emotions play a role in the formation and expression of our identity as well as how our identity changes through the experiences. Our emotions aren't the only factor in our identity, but they play a significant role that is often minimalized because we take for granted that we feel emotions and that they play a role in our identities.

Typically identity is portrayed as a static experience, but while it can be true that certain aspects of identity can become quite fixed, it's also my experience that identity can shift, especially if you are open to it shifting your identity. For example, when you do a magical working to get a result you aren't just getting the result but also changing your identity from what it was before the result, to what it is because you have the result. A lot of the shifting in identity occurs with emotions, because our emotions either help us have realizations around a given structure of identity or become a blockage that defines our identity in a way that isn't helpful.

One of the challenges that we face is learning how not to over identify with our emotions, because the experience of them can be so strong that it can overwhelm a person's identity in the moment. For example if you feel depressed, that emotional experience of depression can take over your identity and impact the experiences you have because of the strength of that feeling. While our emotions aren't our actual identities, it is still all too easy to identify with the emotion because it is expressing the experience we're going through.

The problem with identifying with our emotions is that we can make the mistake of thinking the emotion is our identity, to the point that we don't pay attention to anything else other than the emotion that's being felt. For instance, if you feel the emotion of anxiety and that emotion overwhelms your identity, you may only think of yourself as an anxious person, instead of recognizing other aspects of your identity that are just as important and relevant to who you are, such as your awareness of your identity as a person with a specific background and history that informs who you are.

This isn't to say we should disassociate our identity with our emotions, because that's not a good strategy either (as I'll explain below), but rather we have to find a way to recognize what we feel without letting it overwhelm our sense of identity and our ability to live our lives. When we can acknowledge our emotions without letting them take over who we are, we can place them into the proper context of identity and also release them without becoming them.

Exercise

What emotions do you identify with? How do those emotions shape your awareness of yourself? Are there any emotions that you feel you identify with too much, and if so why?

Share your answers in the Magical Experiments Facebook group with #IAIW.

Your Relationship with Stress

Stress is an everyday reality of life and comes in many forms. We deal with internal stressors in the form of our emotions, reactions, and thoughts, all of which can cause us to feel stress because of how we process and deal with a situation. We deal with external stressors in the form of events and people that intersect with us in our lives. We don't typically have full control of those events or people and so they can become stressors, depending on the nature of the relationship we have with the event or person.

Even a positive experience can bring its own version of stress. You have family come visit, and while it is wonderful to see them, there is also the inevitable stresses that comes with such visits, as you change your schedule to accommodate the people visiting you and also deal with the aspects of them that you don't necessarily care for.

Stress isn't the same as emotions, but it is a contributor to our emotions. I primarily find that stress is a physiological experience that your body has in relationship to the environmental and internal stressors you are dealing with. When you can recognize these stressors for what they are, you can change your relationship with them by defusing your reactions and coming up with behaviors that are more proactive and helpful for helping you handle those stresses.

Sometimes stress culminates in the form of a breakdown, which can cause a person to temporarily go insane. When a breakdown occurs the person may behave differently than they normally would and make changes to their lives because they are trying to escape the stress they are dealing with. It's not a very effective way to deal with stress, because while you may temporarily escape the stress you're dealing with, such changes won't remove you from the stress indefinitely.

One of the benefits of doing internal work is that it can help you work with the stress you're experiencing. You can learn to diffuse and dissolve stress and uncover the root of the stress, so that you can resolve it, instead of allowing it to continue to disturb you.

Exercise

What is your relationship with stress? What types of stresses are you dealing with in your life and how are you handling them?

Share your answers in the Magical Experiments Facebook group with #IAIW.

Your Relationship with Expectations and Attachments

We deal with expectations every day, both our own and other peoples' expectations. We can think of expectations as standards, but they are also attachments to outcomes, wanting something to be a specific way, and not necessarily being open to anything else. I have found that expectations can be blockages in their own right because of how they influence your behavior toward yourself and others. When you have expectations around what you want, for example, it can cause you to miss out on other opportunities because you are only focused on what you want and/or the disappointment you feel when you aren't getting what you want.

I used the word attachments above, because attachments represent our need to have control over something, which in and of itself is an expectation. When we are attached to how a person shows up in our lives, or how a situation is resolved, we are placing expectations on that person or situation, wanting them to confirm to what we want, instead of accepting the person and situation as they are. We can also apply expectations to ourselves, expecting that we will show up a certain way, or act in a certain manner, or otherwise live up to some standard that is usually far too high to reach but has been placed over us as a way of judging ourselves for our own shortcomings.

When we apply internal work to attachments and expectations, what we end up doing is recognizing how they are actually creating suffering in our lives because of how we're fixated on having things be a certain way. We learn to let go of the attachments and expectations and free ourselves from the suffering that accompanies them. We open ourselves to being in the experience instead of trying to define it and as result we may discover more joy than our expectations or attachments could ever bring us.

Exercise

What expectations and attachments do you have? How they affect the experiences you have with yourself, other people, and situations?

Share your answers in the Magical Experiments Facebook group with #IAIW.

Why we try to control our emotions

The opposite response to overly identifying with emotions is trying to control your emotions. When you try to control your emotions this typically takes the form of suppressing your emotions, or dissociating with them. This is also known as compartmentalization, where you box up what you're feeling and it can lead to the creation of emotional blockages. The problem with trying to control your emotions is that inevitably you end up feeling them, but in a way that isn't healthy, or you end up freezing a part of yourself to avoid feeling them. In the former case, you can end up blowing up like a volcano, finally venting all the emotions you've held in, and in the latter case you close yourself off from the emotions you don't want to feel.

We often try to control our emotions because we've been taught that sharing and expressing them is embarrassing or because we find the emotional experience to be uncomfortable. It doesn't help that the emotional state of happiness is emphasized as the state we should all be striving for. Anything other than happiness is treated as abnormal, as if something is wrong with the person for not feeling happy. It should be no surprise then that when people ask how you're doing, the preferred non-answer is "fine" or "ok," because dealing with any other answer causes discomfort for people hearing that someone is unhappy.

The problem with controlling your emotions is that ultimately your efforts to control them don't work. I know this from personal experience because I've tried to box my emotions away and I've also blown up like a volcano. At the same time, I'm not advocating that we simply allow our emotions to dictate our actions and choices. Rather I think it's important to learn how to be present with a given emotional experience without acting on the emotion impulsively or trying to repress the emotion in favor of an artificial state of being. What we must learn to do is become present with our emotions and balance that emotional awareness with other states of knowing that can help us make informed choices in the face of what we're feeling and working through.

Exercise

What is your relationship with your emotions? Do you have a healthy relationship or do you struggle with your emotions and if you struggle how do you work through that struggle?

Share your answers in the Magical Experiments Facebook group with #IAIW.

How do we become present with our emotions?

We become present with our emotions by learning how to accept the emotional experiences we're having, without labeling those experiences as good or bad. At the same time, we accept that the emotional experience is not representative of the totality of our identity. Rather it is an expression of our identity, in the moment, but it's only part of who we are. Your emotions are one state of knowing/being among many that you can experience.

When you feel an emotion, instead of suppressing it or denying it, you breathe into it, and allow yourself to acknowledge and hold space with it. You accept it, but you also accept that it is a temporary experience. You will feel the emotion in the moment, but not allow it to define the totality of your being. You also recognize the relationship between your thoughts and emotions and how each feeds the other, which can trap you in recursive loops of obsession, and also stops you from being truly present with the emotion.

Being present with our emotions also involves experiential embodiment. Experiential embodiment is a process where you pay attention to how your body communicates with you through the experienced sensations that come through your sensorial awareness. Your emotions are one type of experienced sensation that your body feels, but this sensation can be translated into thoughts which may cause us to ignore the original sensation in favor our attempts to rationalize or otherwise explain what is being experienced. If we were to instead simply be present with the experience, without having to try and explain it away, we would open ourselves to be more fully in that experience and allowing it to transform us in the moment, as opposed to continually holding onto it with our thoughts.

Being present with your emotions really involves learning how to embrace and let go of the emotion in the moment. When we do this, we don't create internal tensions and blockages. Instead we take on the energetic experience and use it in the moment without creating attachments to it. We recognize that the present is transitory, just a moment in a life of moments that we can be in and also use in our magical work, both for practical results and for internal work.

Conclusion

In this chapter we've introduced internal work in relationship to the issues that internal work is typically done around. I wouldn't be surprised if some of you, in reading this chapter, would think that internal work is primarily psychological. While there is a psychological component to internal work, what we're going to discover is that there is much more going on with internal work than psychology. Internal work has physiological and energetic components, which we're going to explore in more depth over the rest of the book. My goal is to provide you access to the tools, techniques, and processes that you can employ to help you resolve internal issues, and consequently make your life much simpler.

There is one thing I must say about internal work. It is not a cure all for the internal issues you are dealing with. It is a set of tools and techniques that can help you work with your internal issues, but you shouldn't hesitate to get professional help if you need it, in conjunction with doing internal work. I have done internal work in conjunction with therapy and found that doing the two together has been helpful. Sometimes doing internal work will also cause you to experience states of being more intensely. For example, when I've done internal work around trauma I've experienced, I have initially felt more depressed because the trauma isn't a wonderful subject to be dealing with. I have ultimately benefitted from doing the internal work, but I've also accepted that I may sometimes, in the pursuit of it, feel emotions and experiences that need to be accepted and worked through in order to release the trauma as much as possible.

With that said, let's explore the techniques and practices of internal work and see how they can be applied to your life in a meaningful way that helps you resolve your own internal issues and conflicts.

Want to learn more inner alchemy?

Get Inner Alchemy of Internal Work, available through my website[1] and with retailers[2].

---

1.   https://www.magicalexperiments.com/inner-alchemy-series

2.   https://books2read.com/u/47QOxN

Learn How Magic Works. Get the Process of Magic!

In the Process of Magic I explain how Magic works and how you can use it to achieve consistent results in your life. I'll walk you through the principles of magic, and you'll learn how to design your own magical workings.

Available in print and on any digital e-book format. Visit https://www.magicalexperiments.com/how-magic-works-series/ to get your copy today!

Get the Magical Journals of Taylor Ellwood

My magical journals are a collection of articles, blog entries, and personal musings about magic, where I share my work in progress. If you want to learn how magic works, reading these journals can show you the work in progress of a magician, which can be a valuable to way to learn magic. You can pick them up at any e-book retailer. To learn more visit https://www.magicalexperiments.com/magical-journals-of-taylor-ellwood

Learn how Pop Culture Magic Works

Magick for geeks! *Pop Culture Magick* is about a new approach to doing magick. Taylor Ellwood recognize that in this day and age the truly flexible magician is the magician who adapts with the times. *Pop Culture Magick* is a reflection of this need for adaptation. Ideas for practical magick can come from many unusual sources and pop culture is one such source. *Pop Culture Magick* walks you through how to apply pop culture to your magical practices.

Available in print and on any digital e-book format. Visit https://www.magicalexperiments.com/pop-culture-magic-series/ to get your copy today!

Don't miss out!

Visit the website below and you can sign up to receive emails whenever Taylor Ellwood publishes a new book. There's no charge and no obligation.

https://books2read.com/r/B-A-MUJG-GOYX

BOOKS 2 READ

Connecting independent readers to independent writers.

About the Author

Taylor Ellwood is a quirky and eccentric magician who's written the Process of Magic, Pop Culture Magic, and Space/Time Magic. Recently Taylor has also started writing fiction and is releasing his first Superhero Novel, Learning How to Fly later this year. He's insatiably curious about how magic works and loves spinning a good yarn.

For more information about his latest magical work visit http://www.magicalexperiments.com

For more information about his latest fiction visit http://www.imagineyourreality.com

Read more at www.magicalexperiments.com.

Milton Keynes UK
Ingram Content Group UK Ltd.
UKHW010641021023
429777UK00001B/67